This book belongs to

Test color page

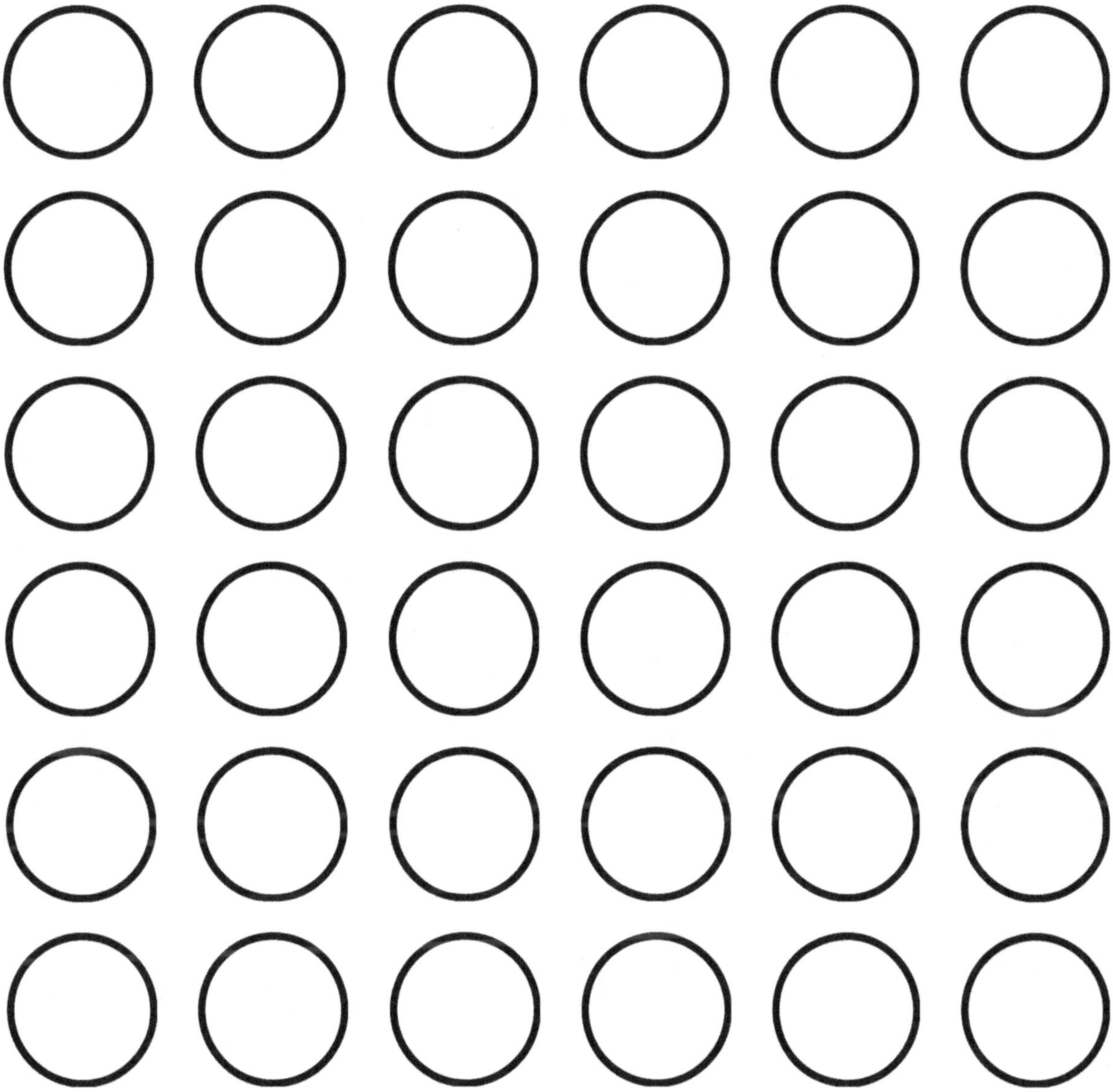

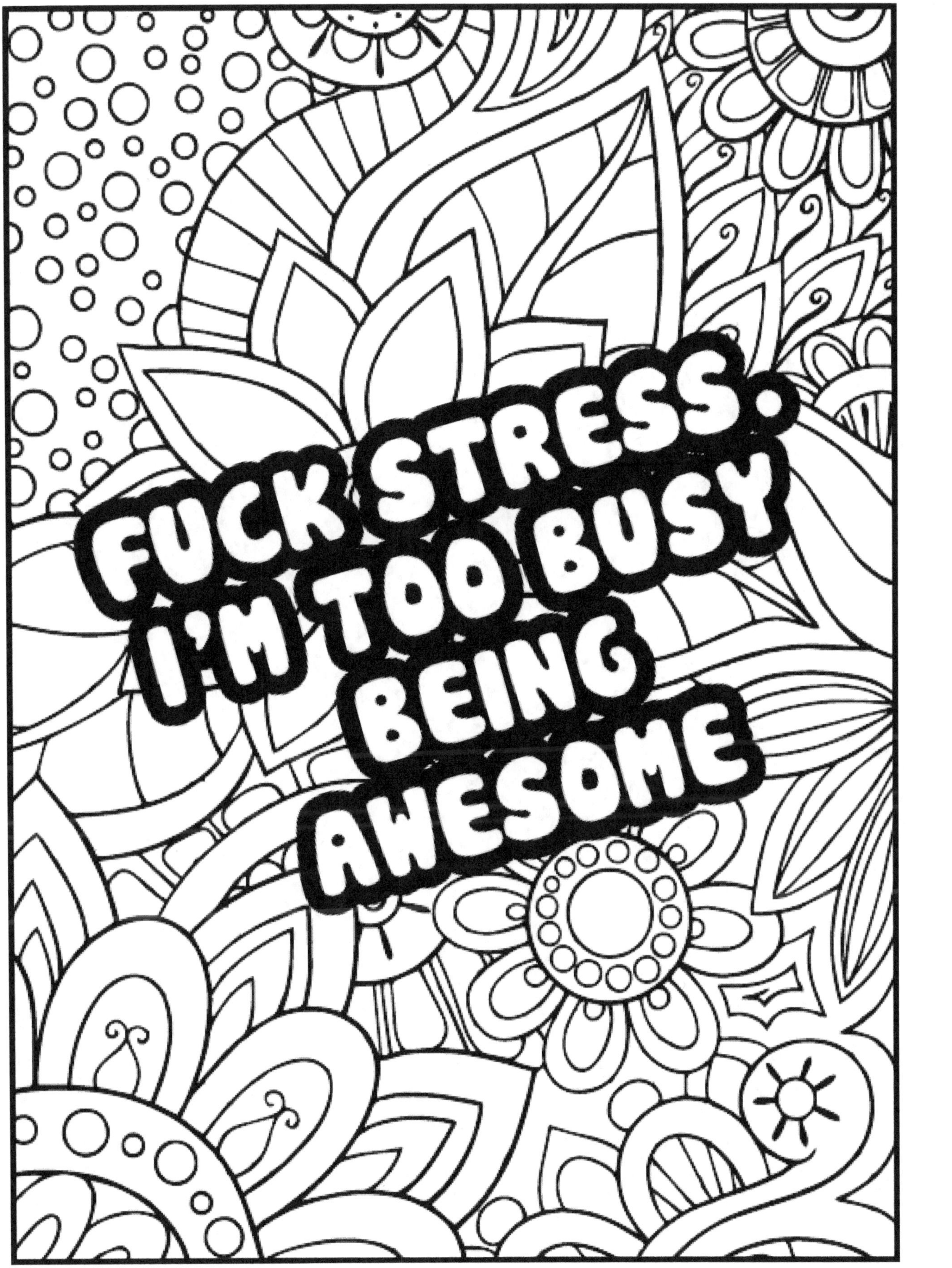
FUCK STRESS.
I'M TOO BUSY
BEING
AWESOME

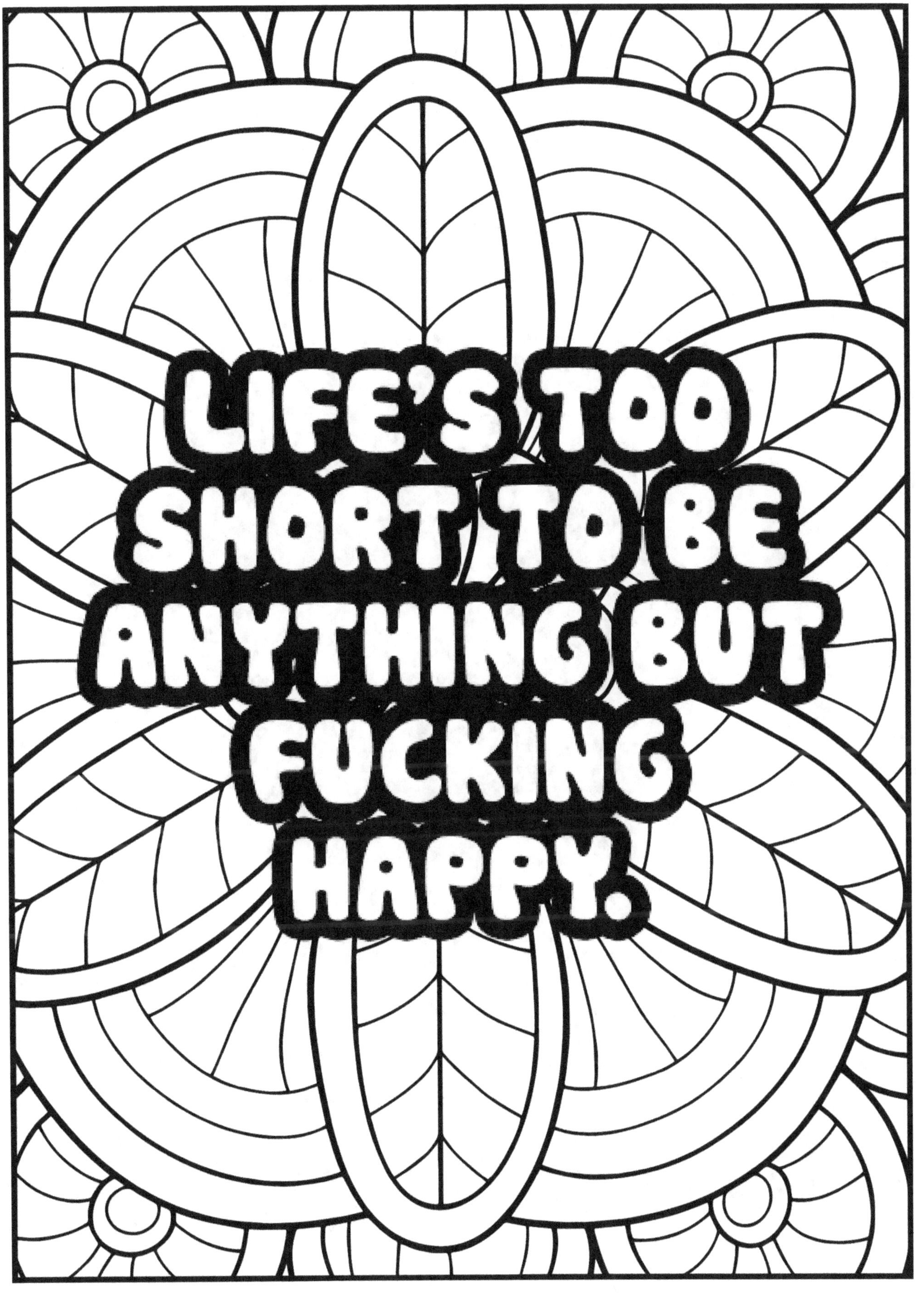
LIFE'S TOO
SHORT TO BE
ANYTHING BUT
FUCKING
HAPPY.

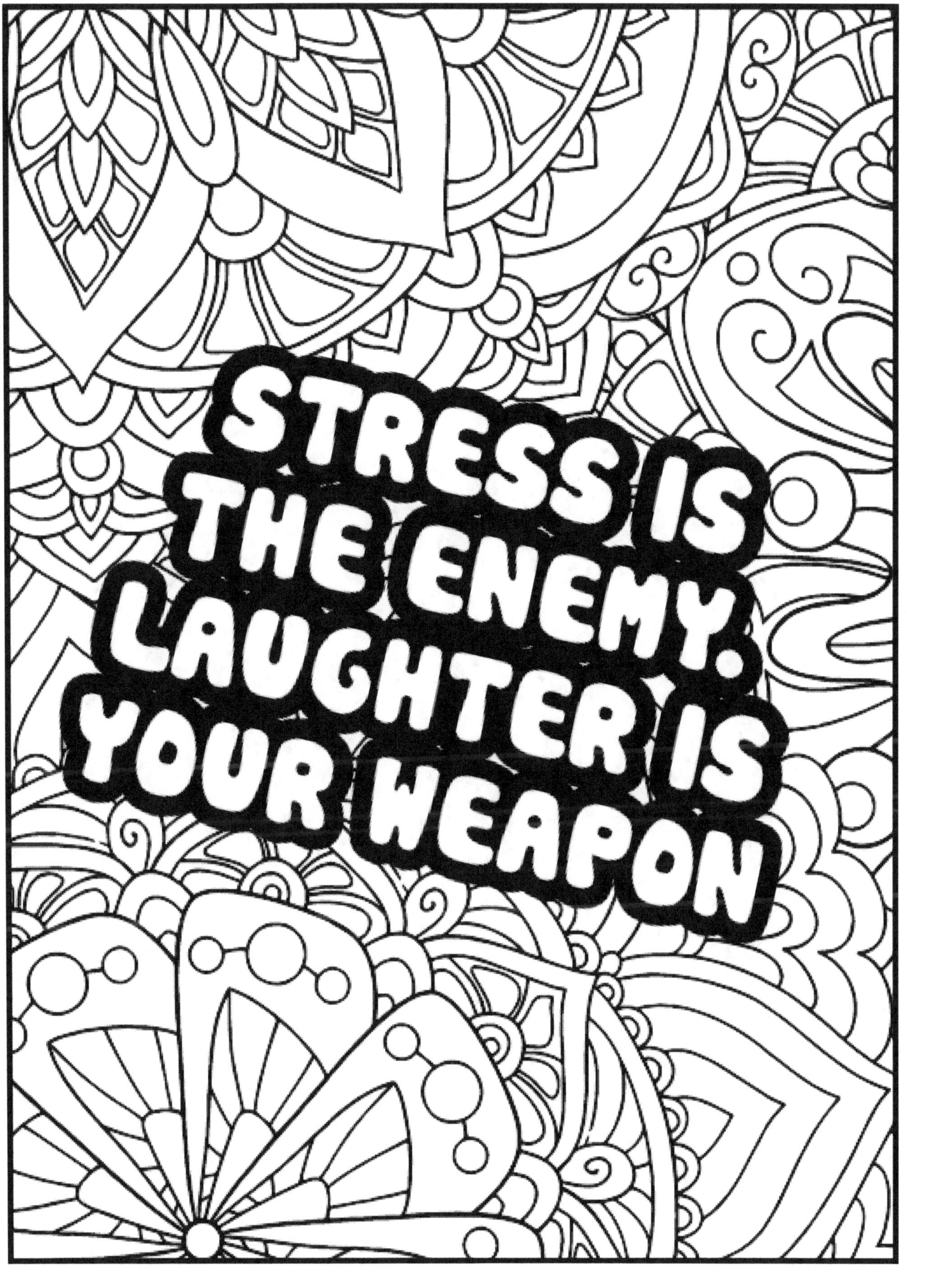
STRESS IS
THE ENEMY.
LAUGHTER IS
YOUR WEAPON

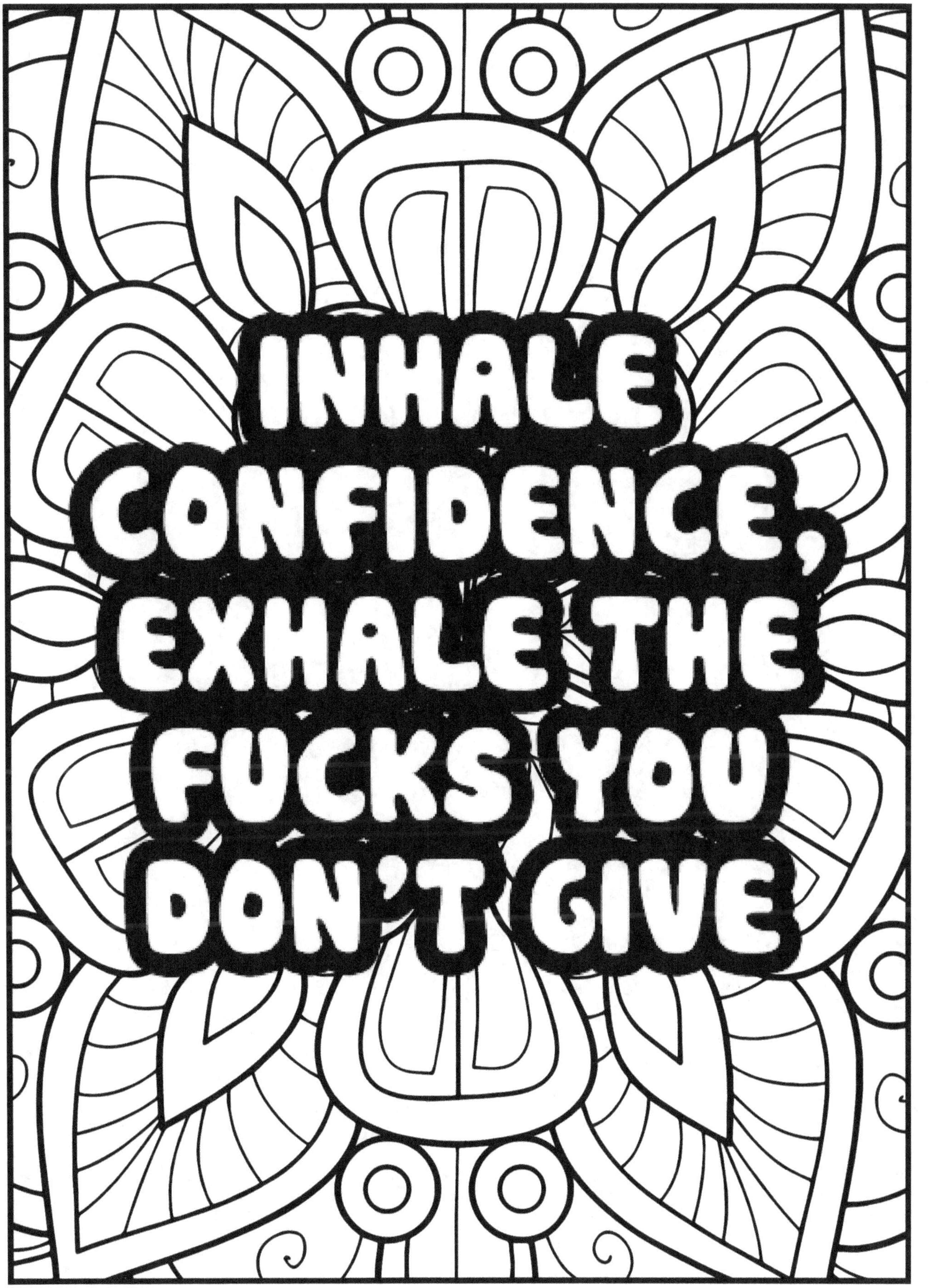
INHALE
CONFIDENCE,
EXHALE THE
FUCKS YOU
DON'T GIVE

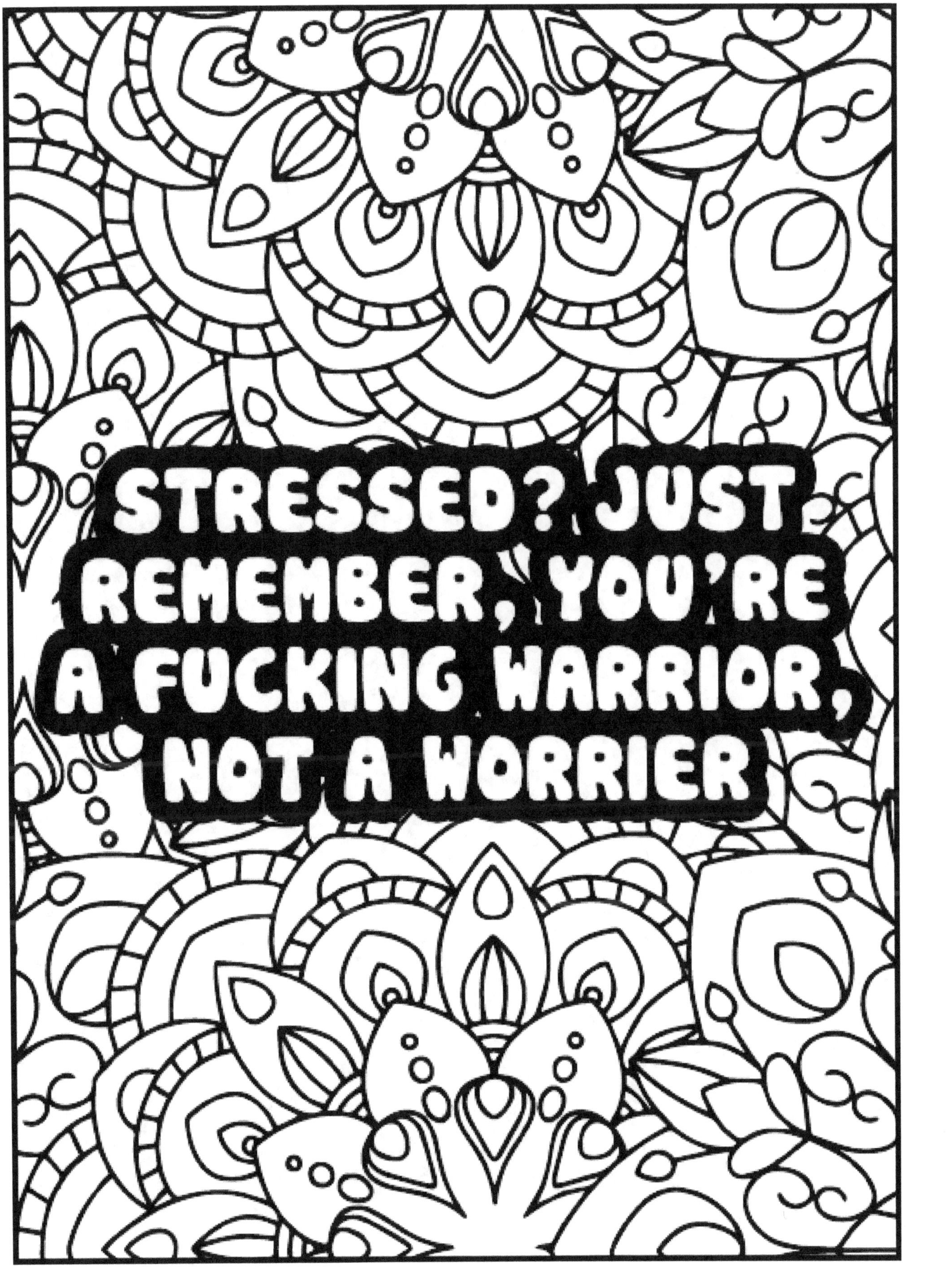
STRESSED? JUST REMEMBER, YOU'RE A FUCKING WARRIOR, NOT A WORRIER

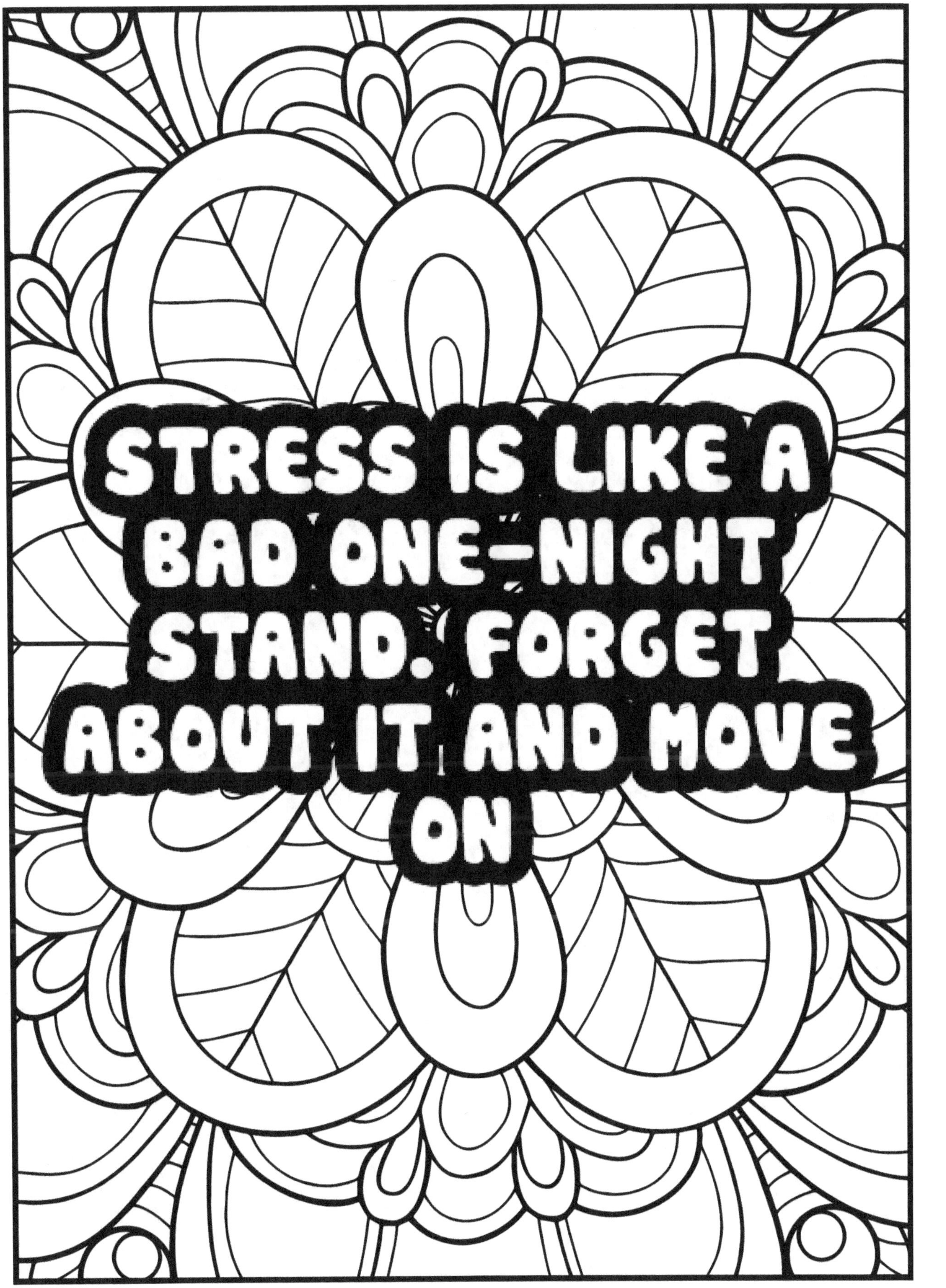
STRESS IS LIKE A BAD ONE-NIGHT STAND. FORGET ABOUT IT AND MOVE ON

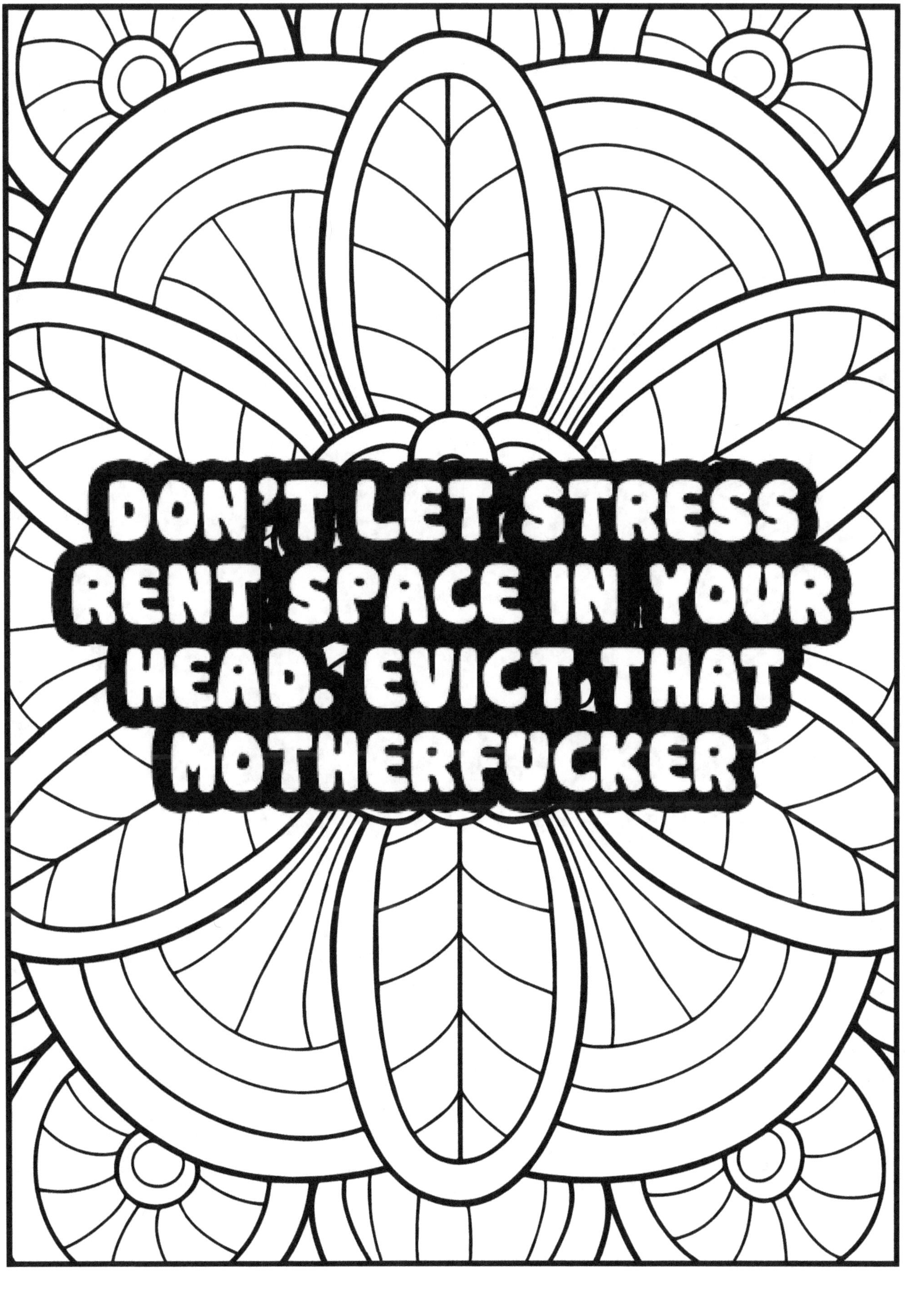
DON'T LET STRESS
RENT SPACE IN YOUR
HEAD. EVICT THAT
MOTHERFUCKER

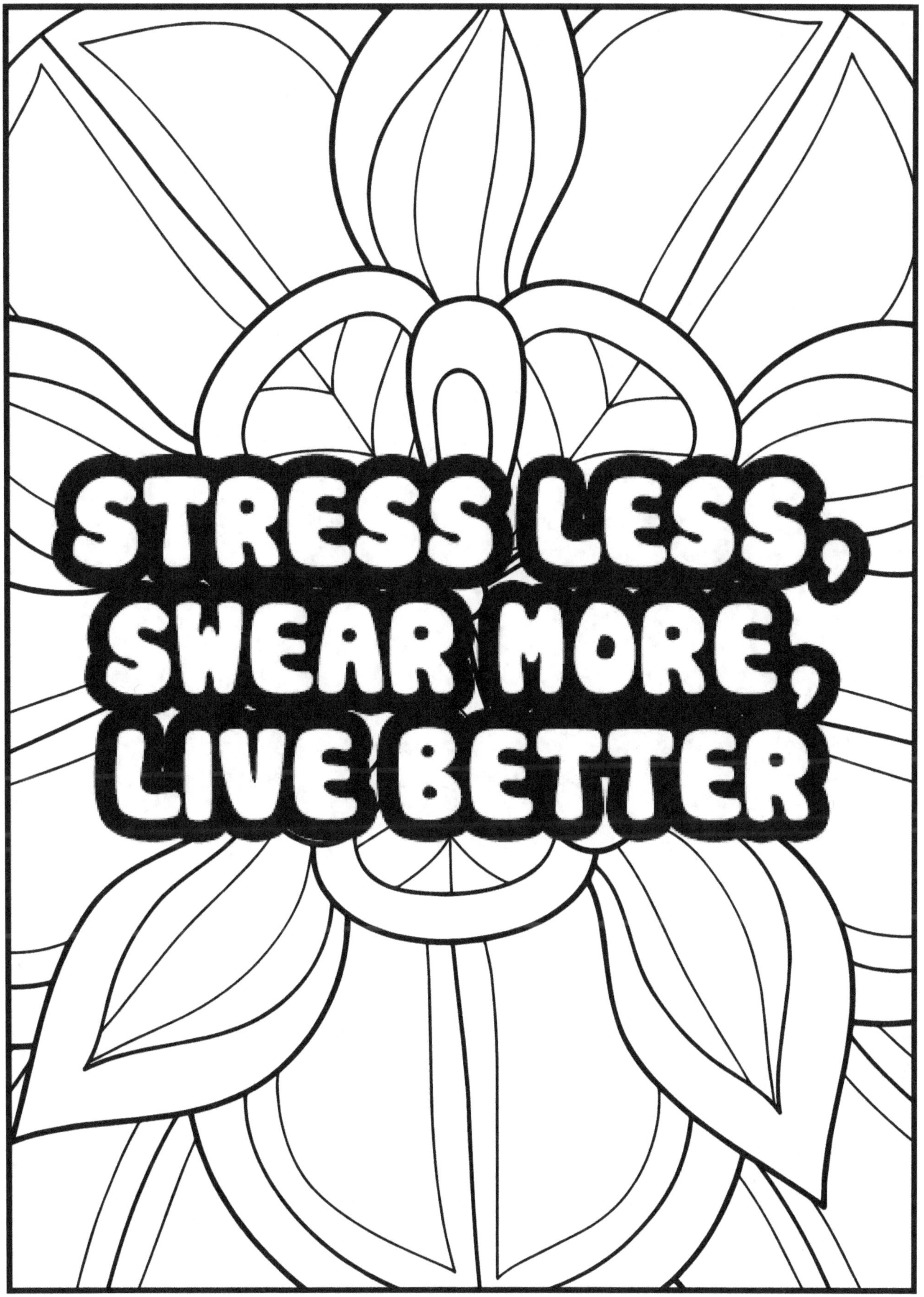
STRESS LESS,
SWEAR MORE,
LIVE BETTER

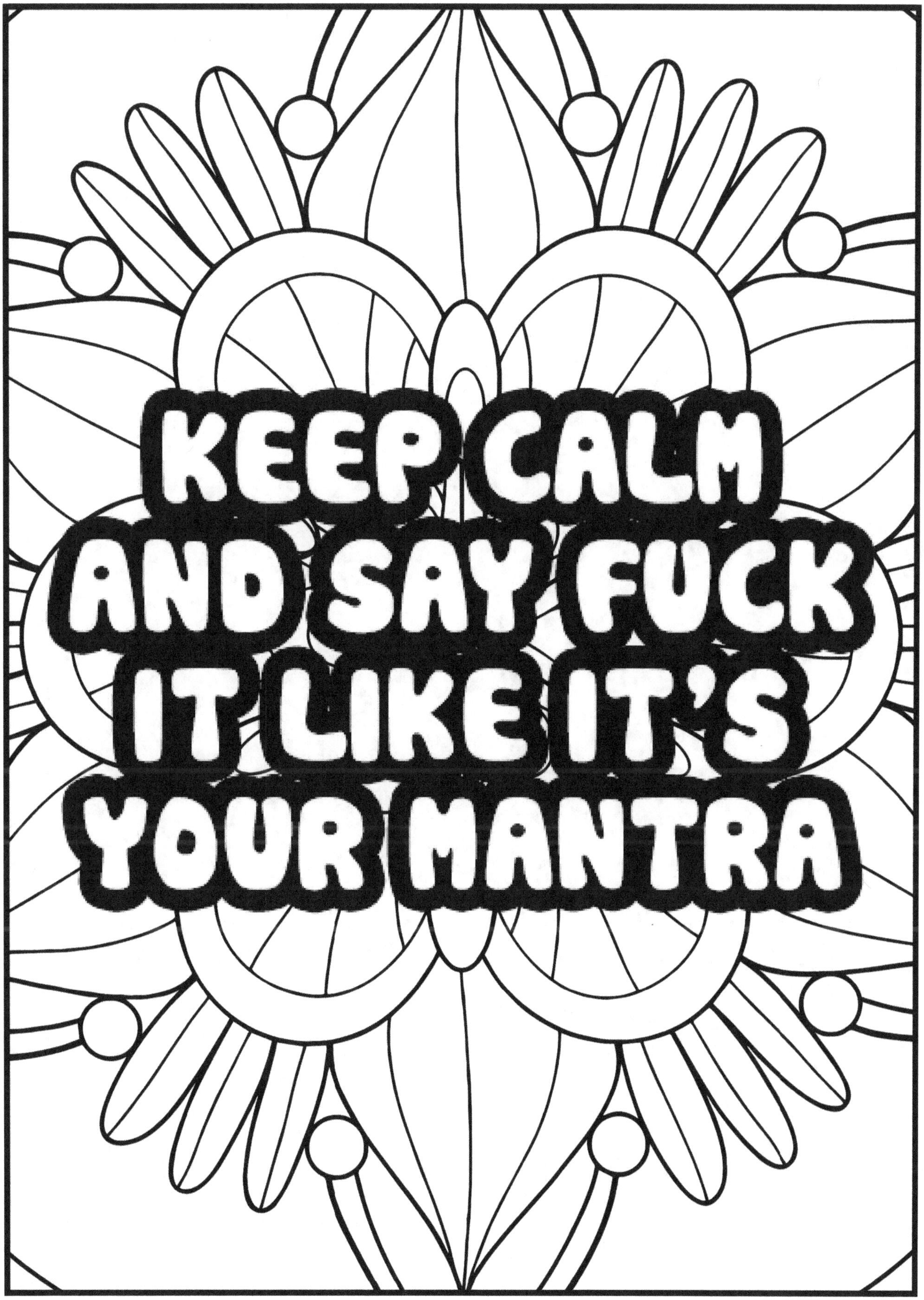
KEEP CALM
AND SAY FUCK
IT LIKE IT'S
YOUR MANTRA

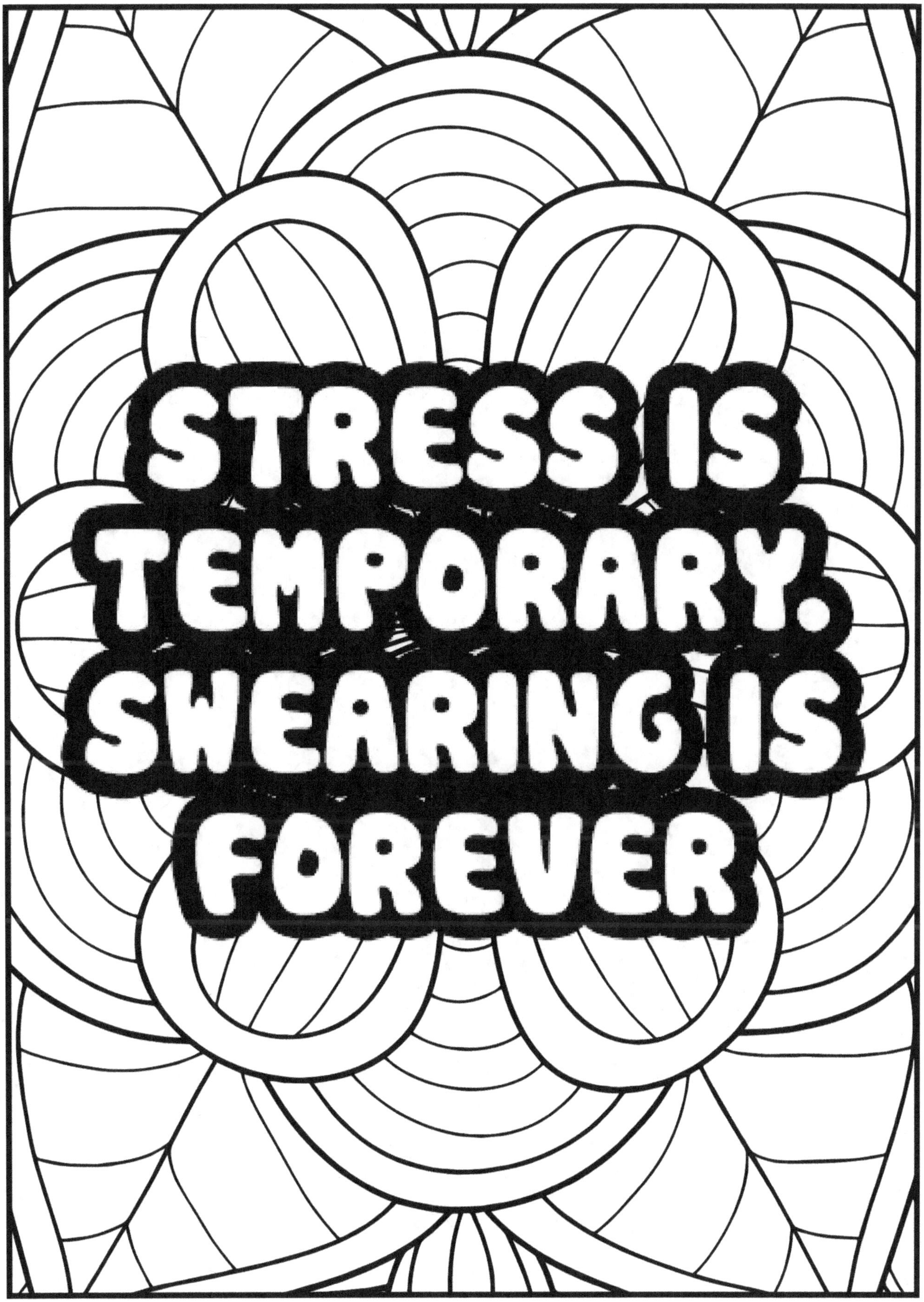
STRESS IS
TEMPORARY.
SWEARING IS
FOREVER

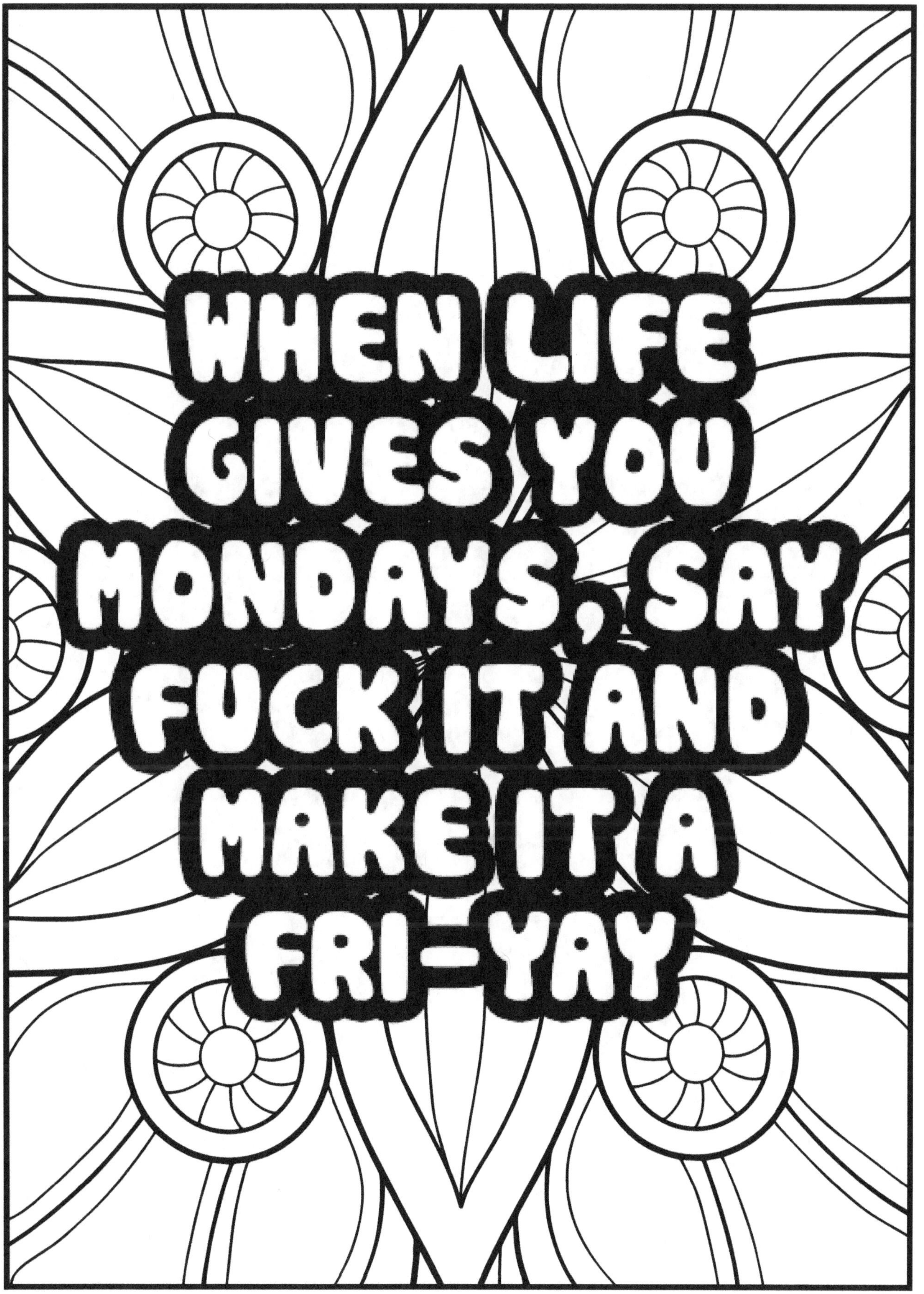
WHEN LIFE
GIVES YOU
MONDAYS, SAY
FUCK IT AND
MAKE IT A
FRI-YAY

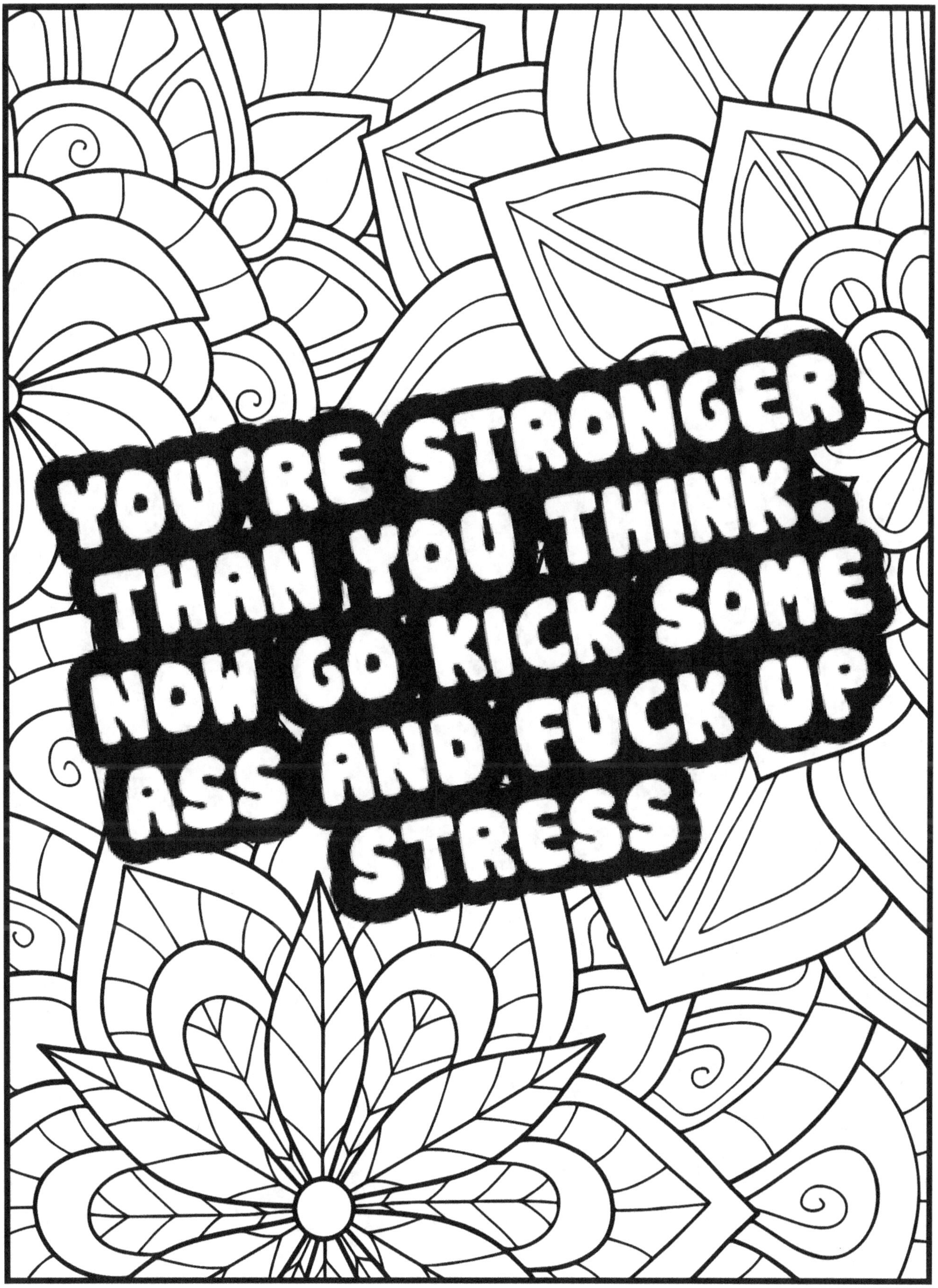
YOU'RE STRONGER
THAN YOU THINK.
NOW GO KICK SOME
ASS AND FUCK UP
STRESS

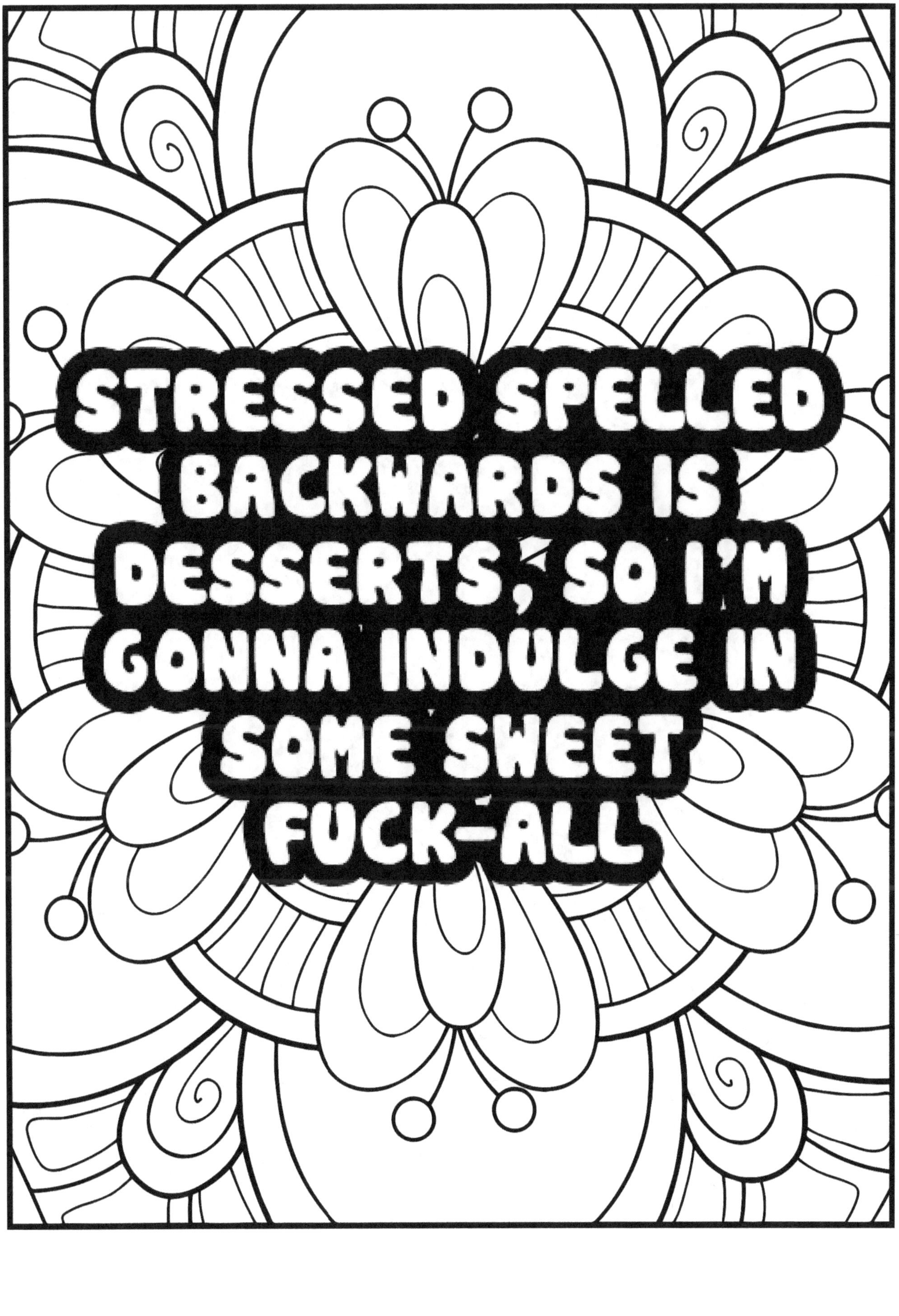
STRESSED SPELLED BACKWARDS IS DESSERTS, SO I'M GONNA INDULGE IN SOME SWEET FUCK-ALL

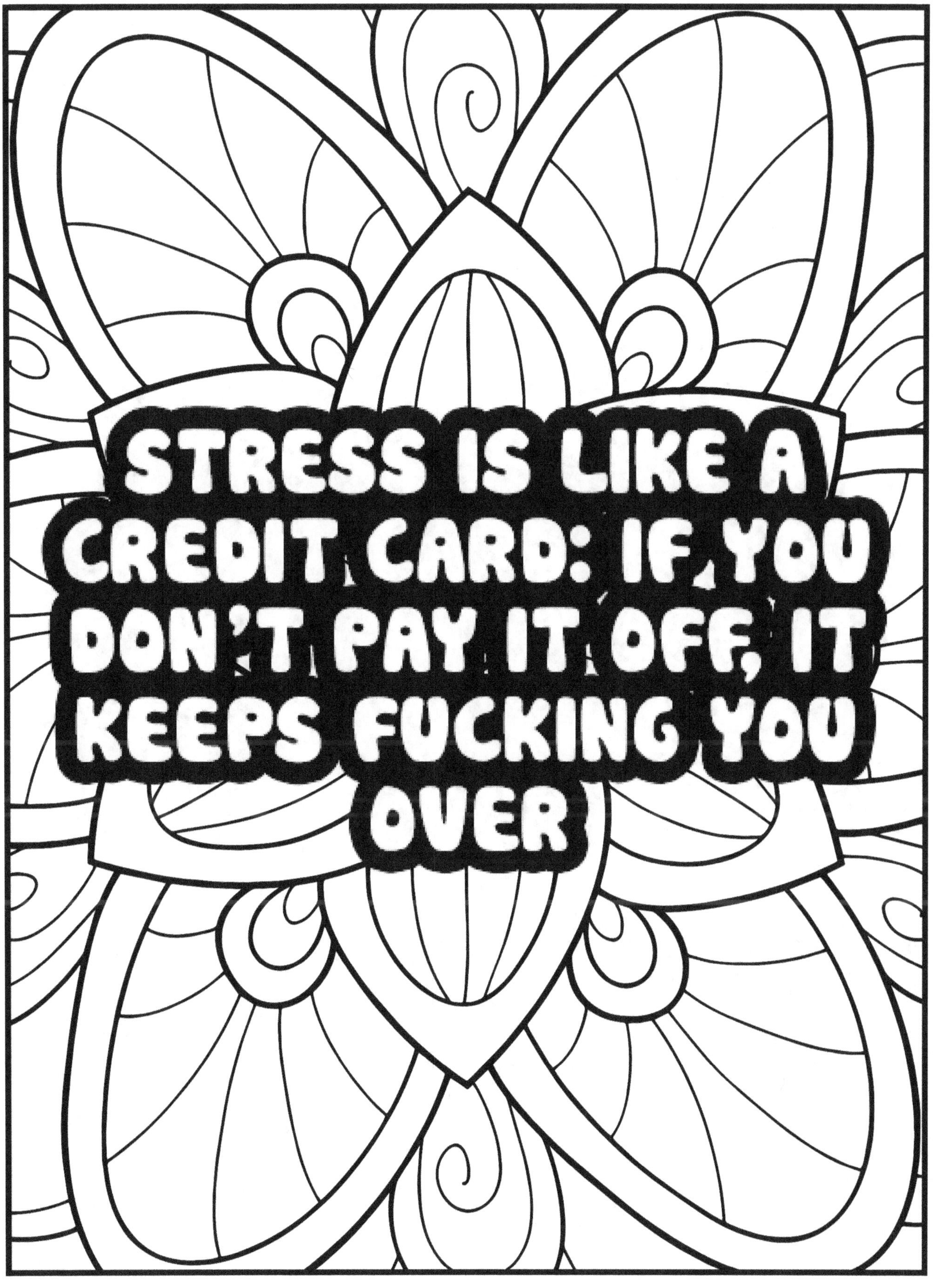
STRESS IS LIKE A CREDIT CARD: IF YOU DON'T PAY IT OFF, IT KEEPS FUCKING YOU OVER

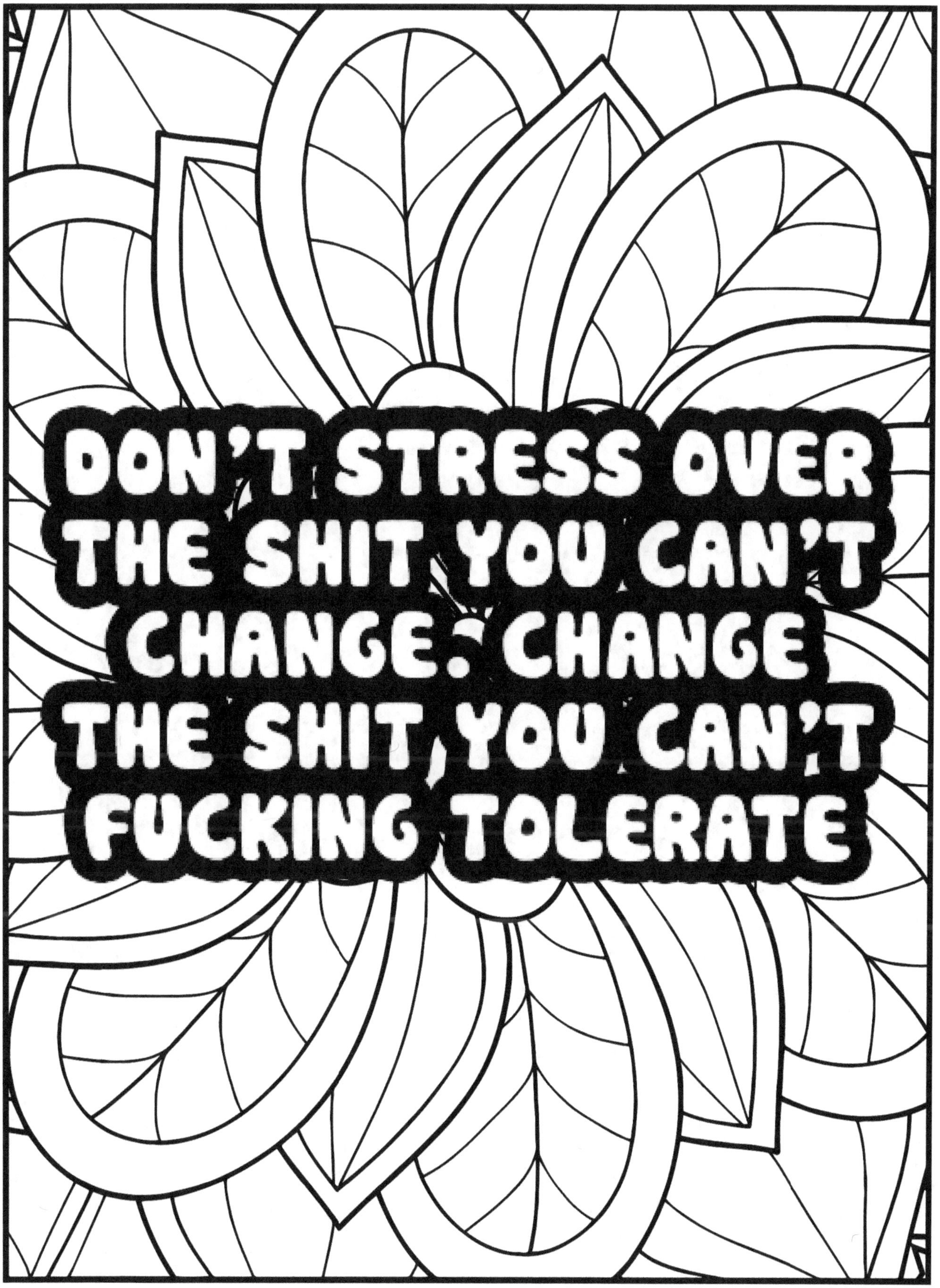
DON'T STRESS OVER
THE SHIT YOU CAN'T
CHANGE. CHANGE
THE SHIT YOU CAN'T
FUCKING TOLERATE

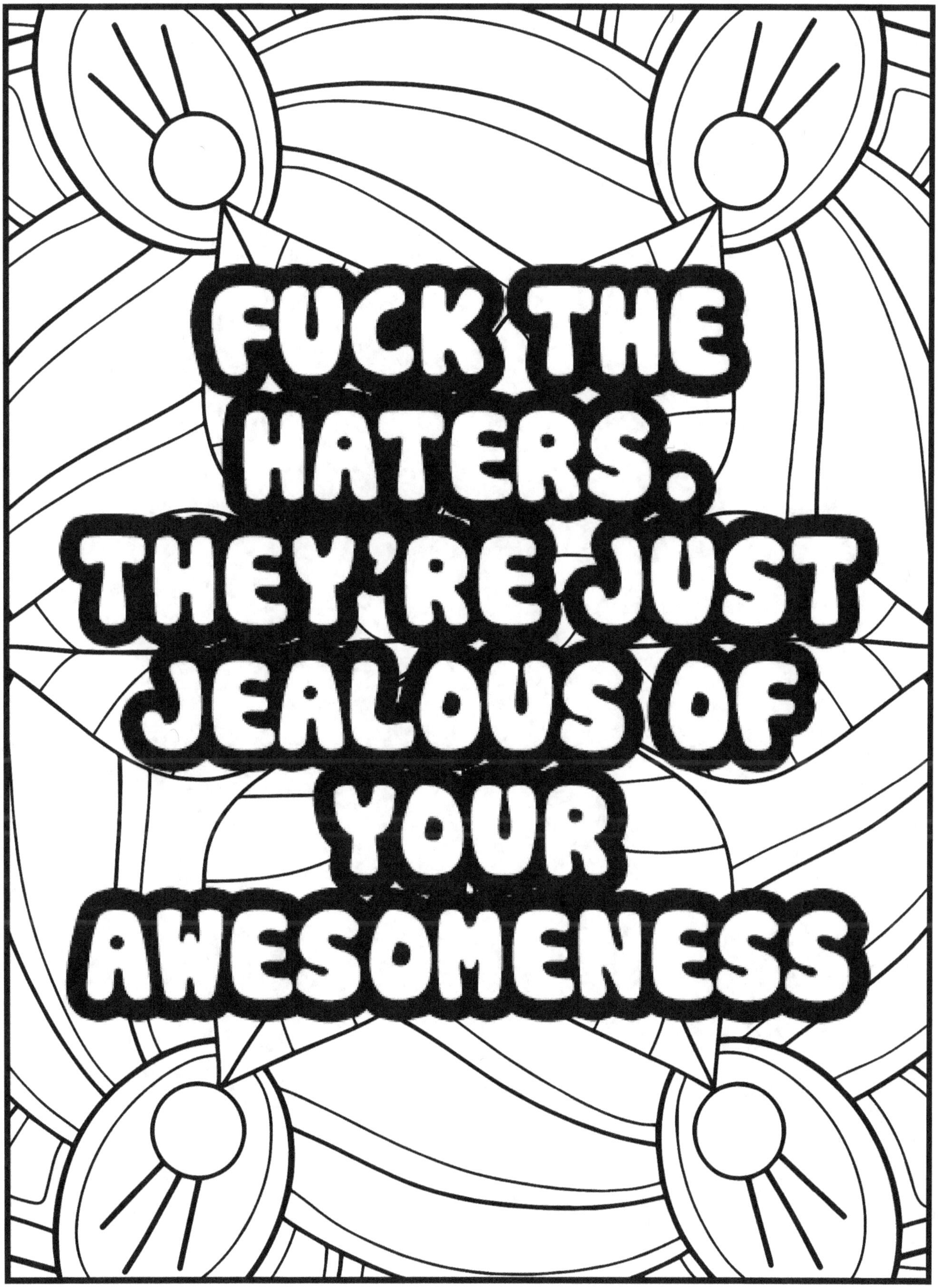
FUCK THE HATERS. THEY'RE JUST JEALOUS OF YOUR AWESOMENESS

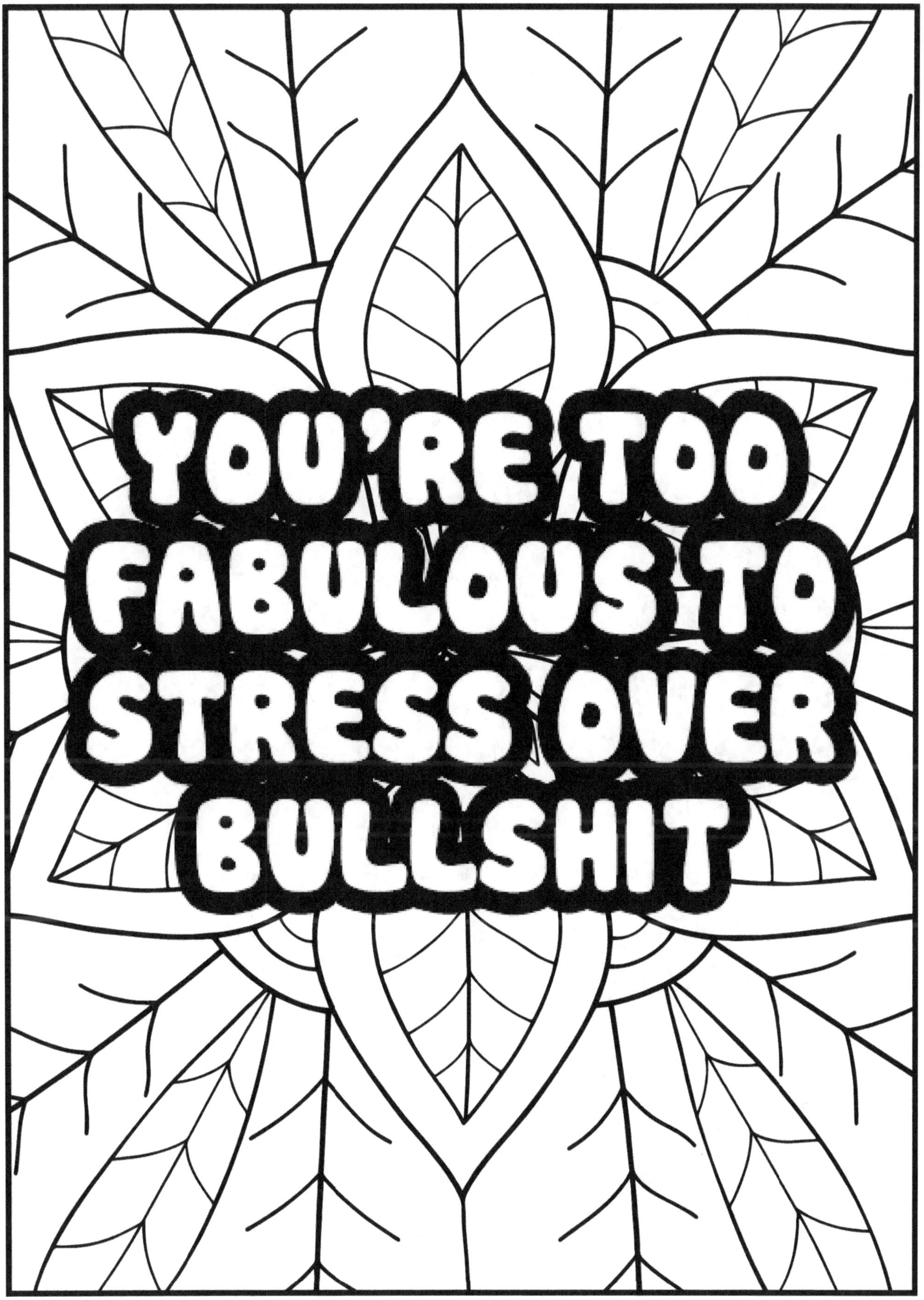
YOU'RE TOO FABULOUS TO STRESS OVER BULLSHIT

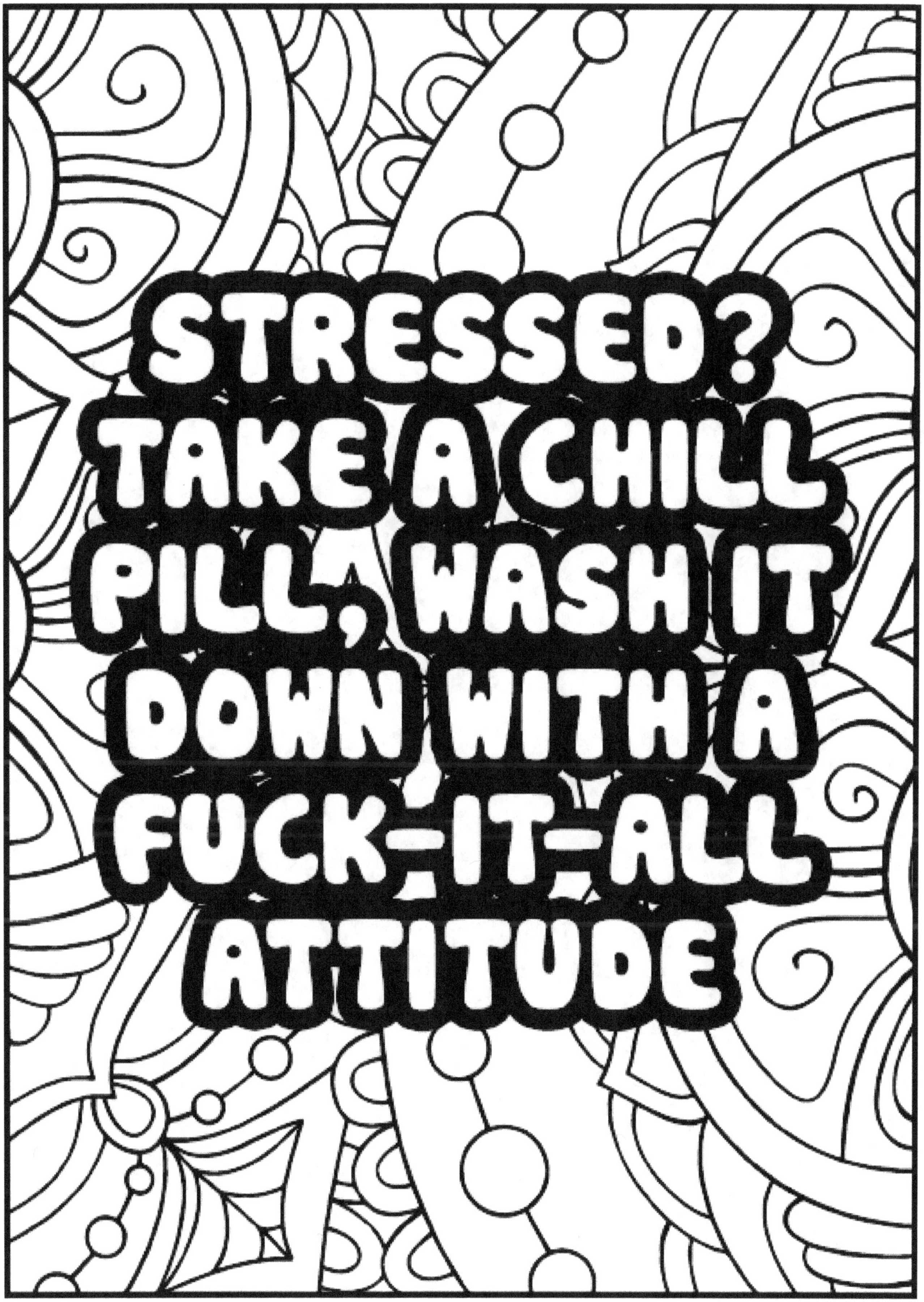
STRESSED?
TAKE A CHILL
PILL, WASH IT
DOWN WITH A
FUCK-IT-ALL
ATTITUDE

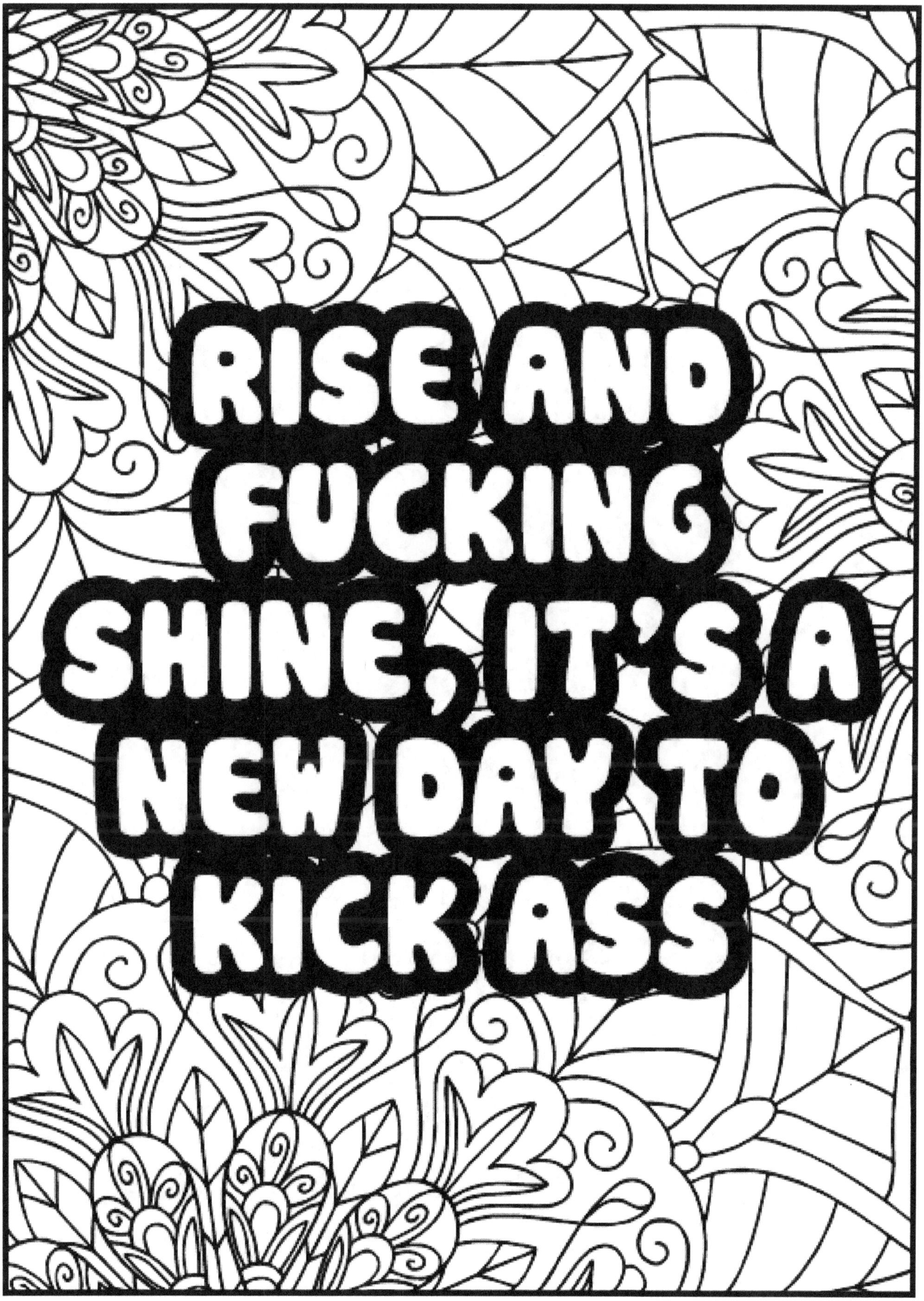
RISE AND
FUCKING
SHINE, IT'S A
NEW DAY TO
KICK ASS

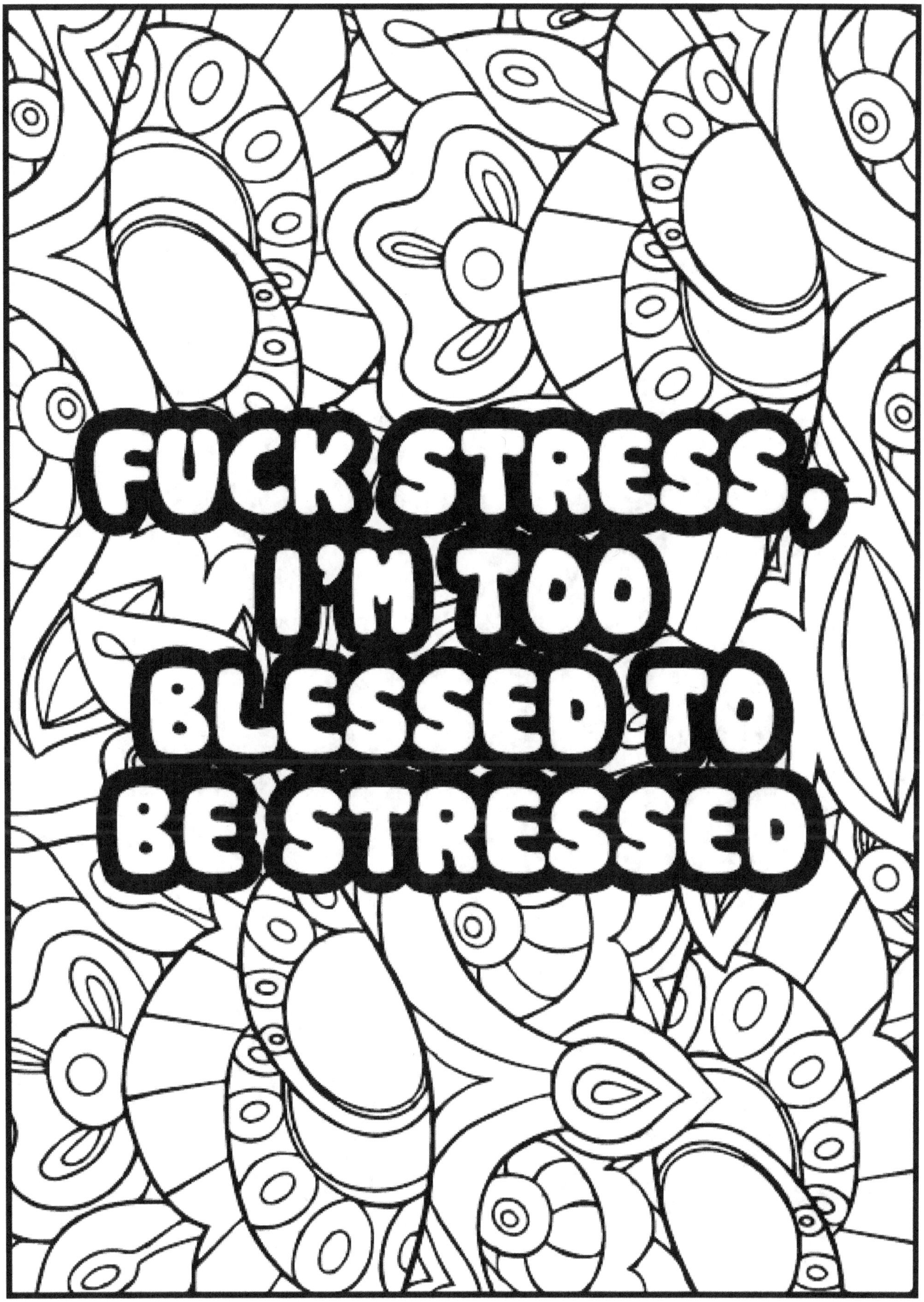
FUCK STRESS,
I'M TOO
BLESSED TO
BE STRESSED

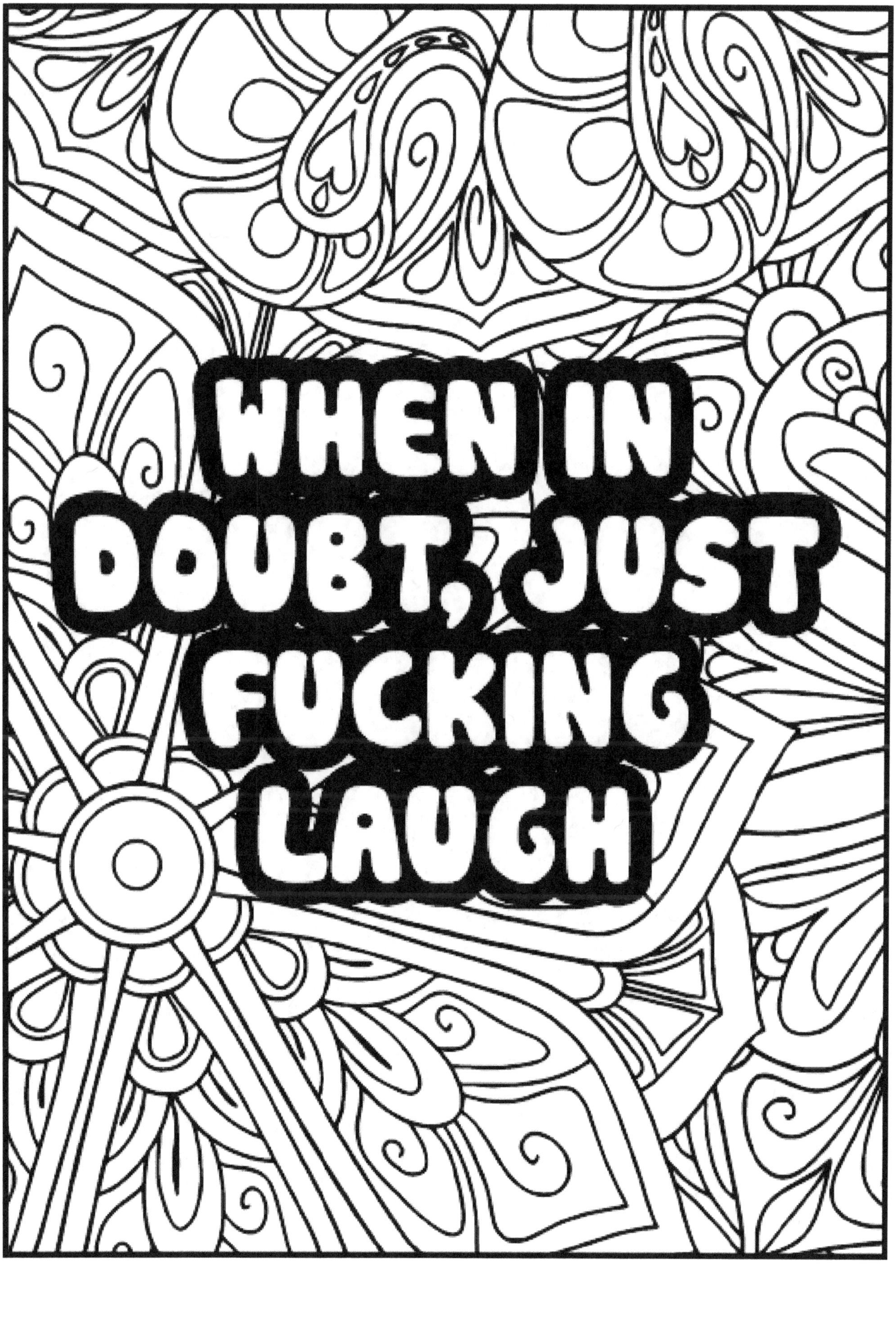
WHEN IN DOUBT, JUST FUCKING LAUGH

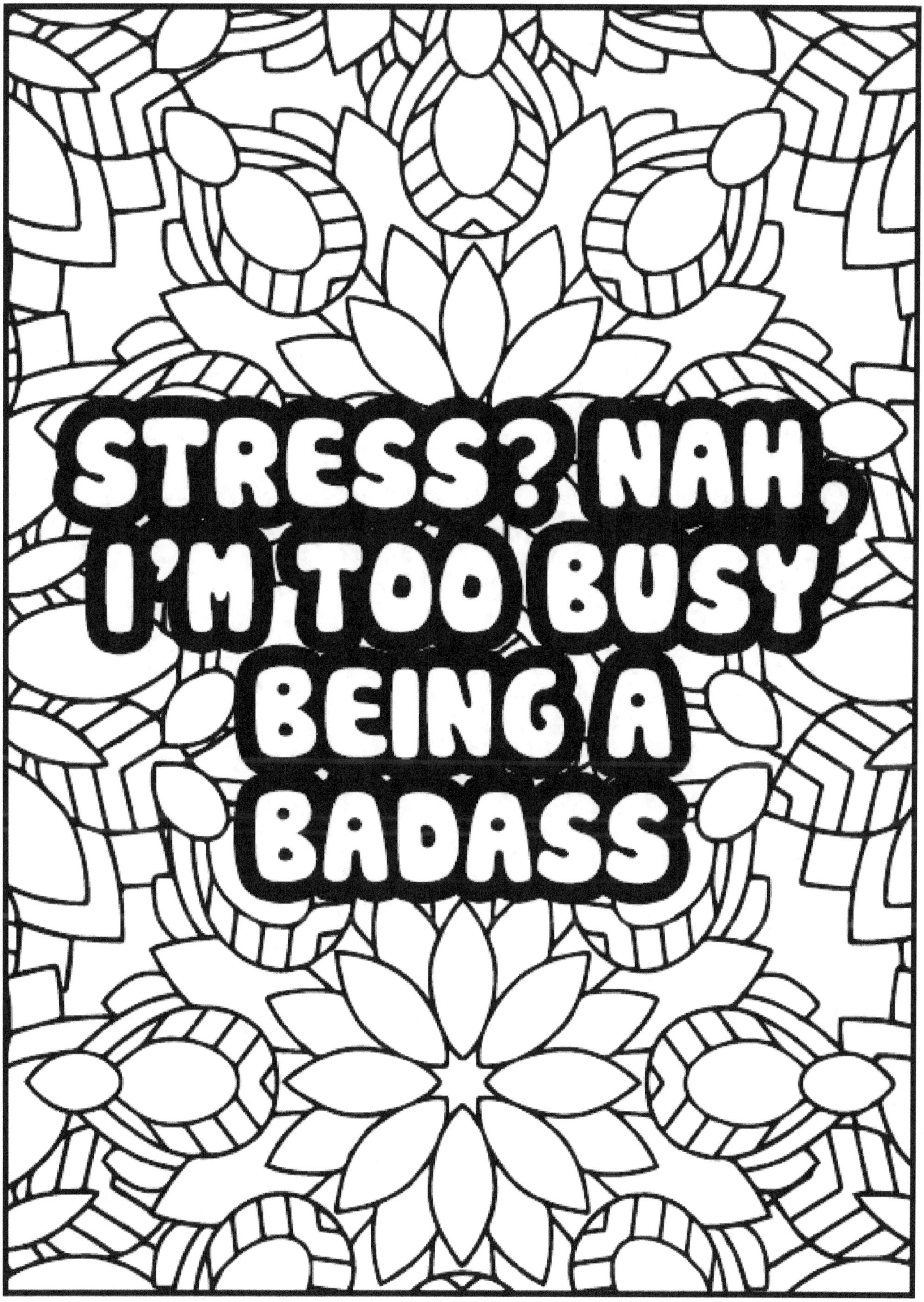
STRESS? NAH,
I'M TOO BUSY
BEING A
BADASS

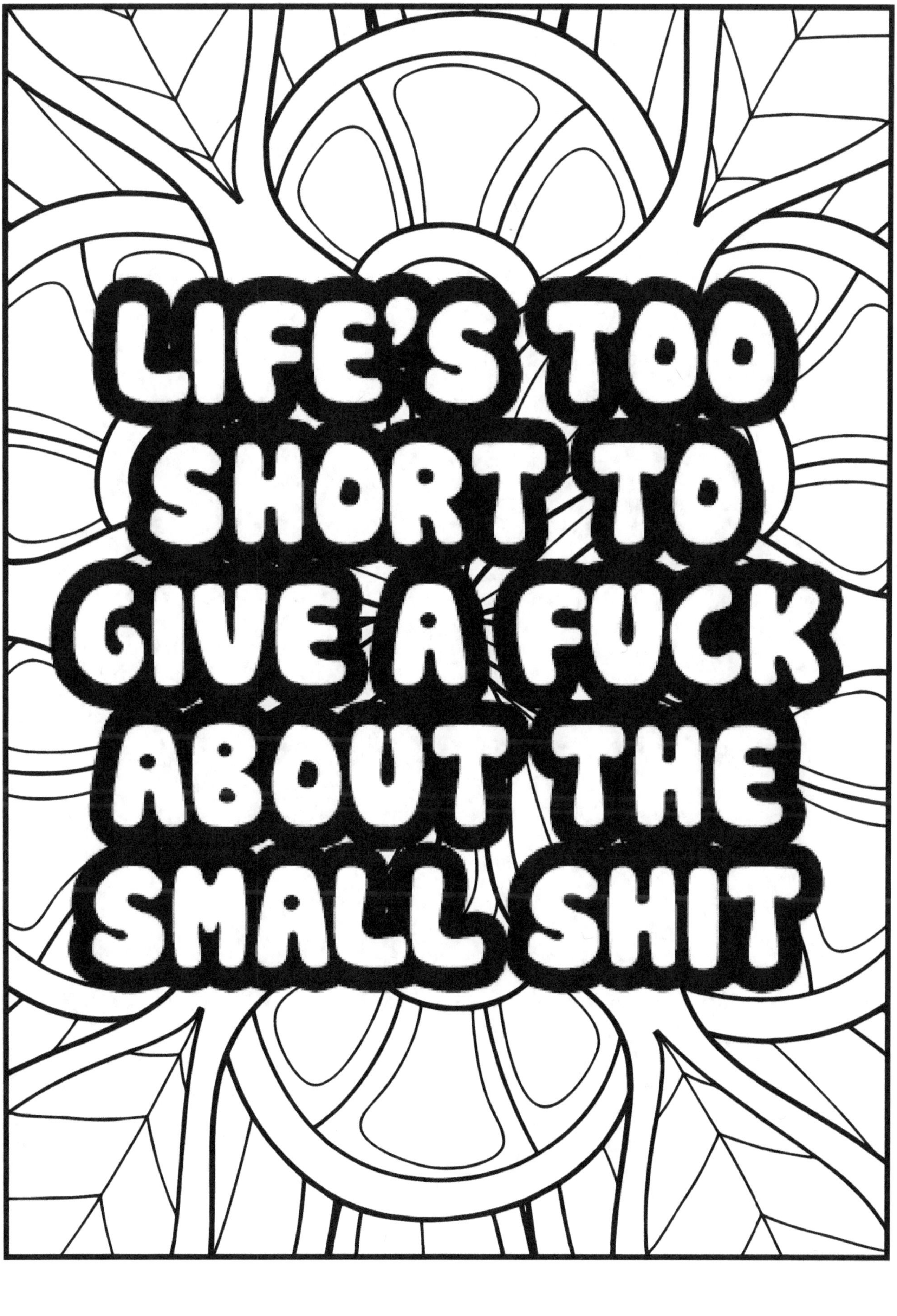
LIFE'S TOO
SHORT TO
GIVE A FUCK
ABOUT THE
SMALL SHIT

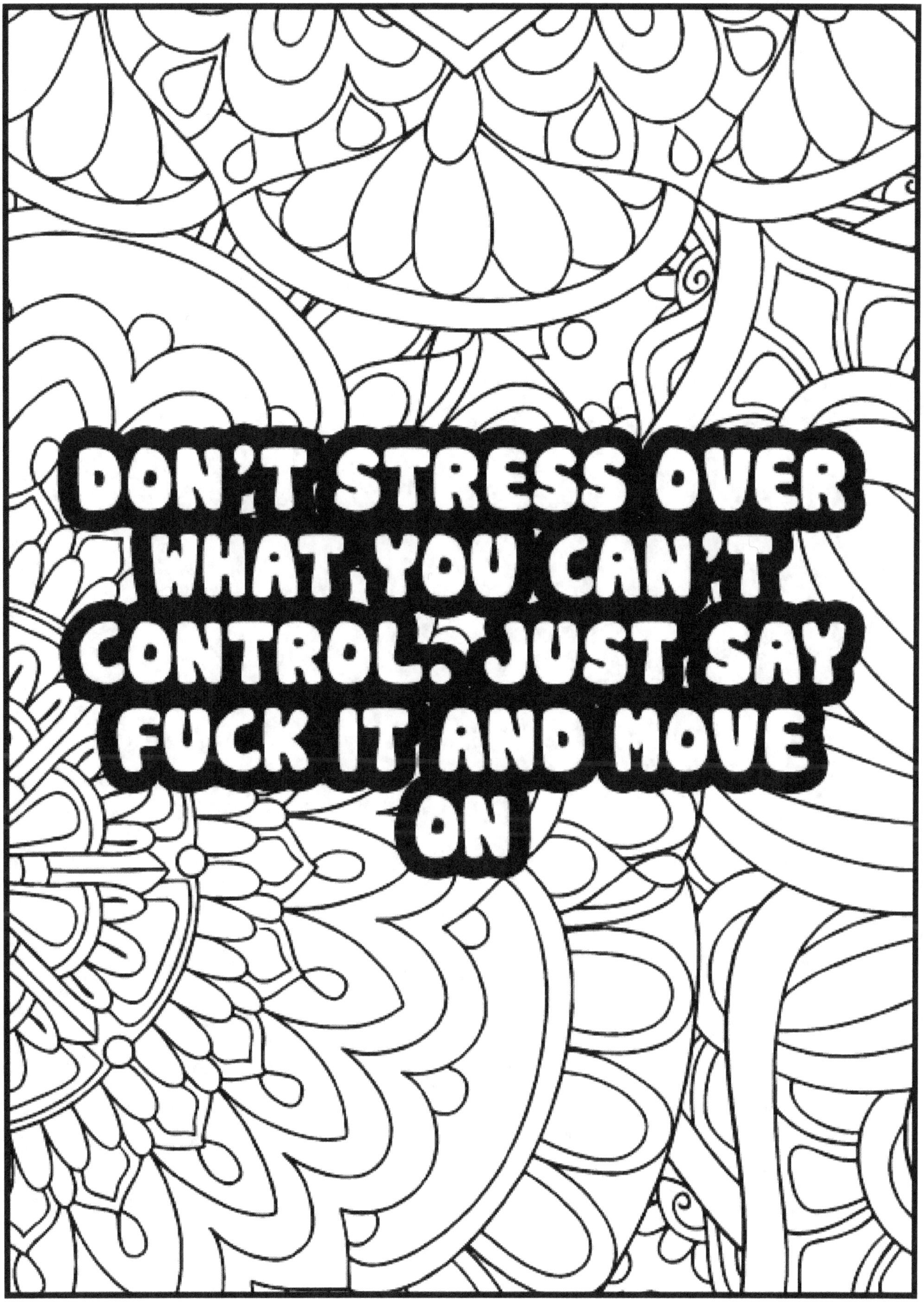
DON'T STRESS OVER WHAT YOU CAN'T CONTROL. JUST SAY FUCK IT AND MOVE ON

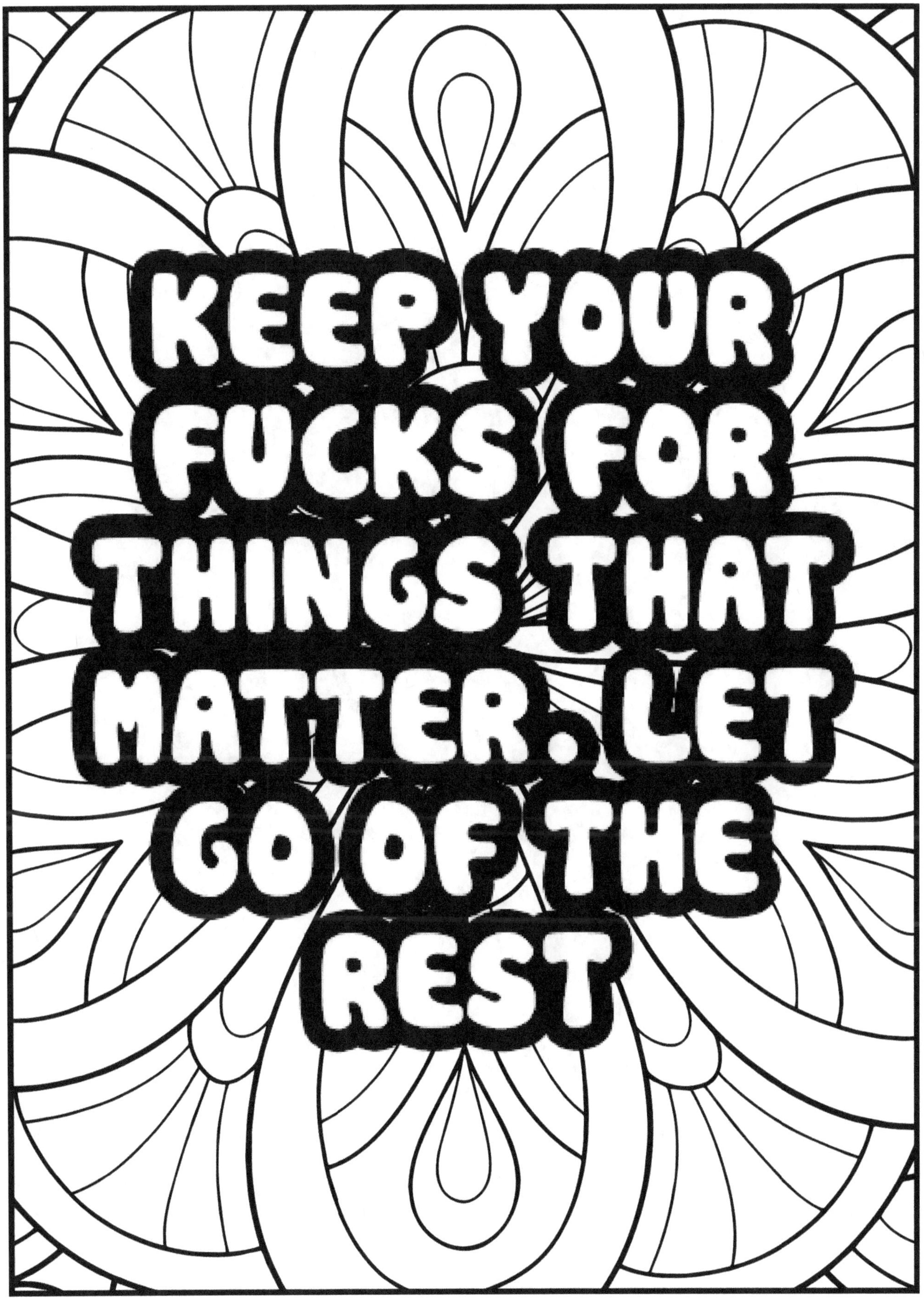
KEEP YOUR FUCKS FOR THINGS THAT MATTER. LET GO OF THE REST

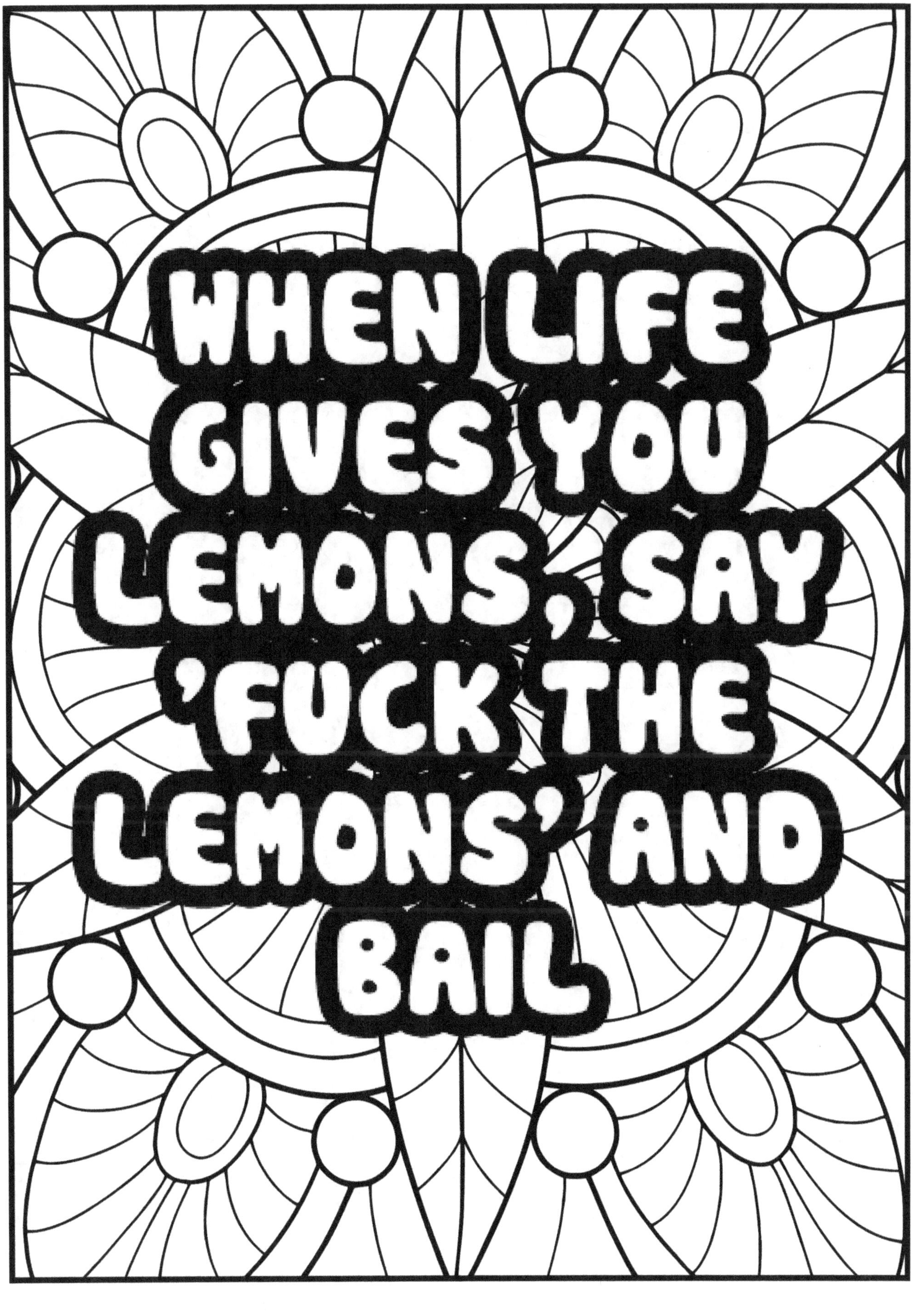
WHEN LIFE GIVES YOU LEMONS, SAY 'FUCK THE LEMONS' AND BAIL

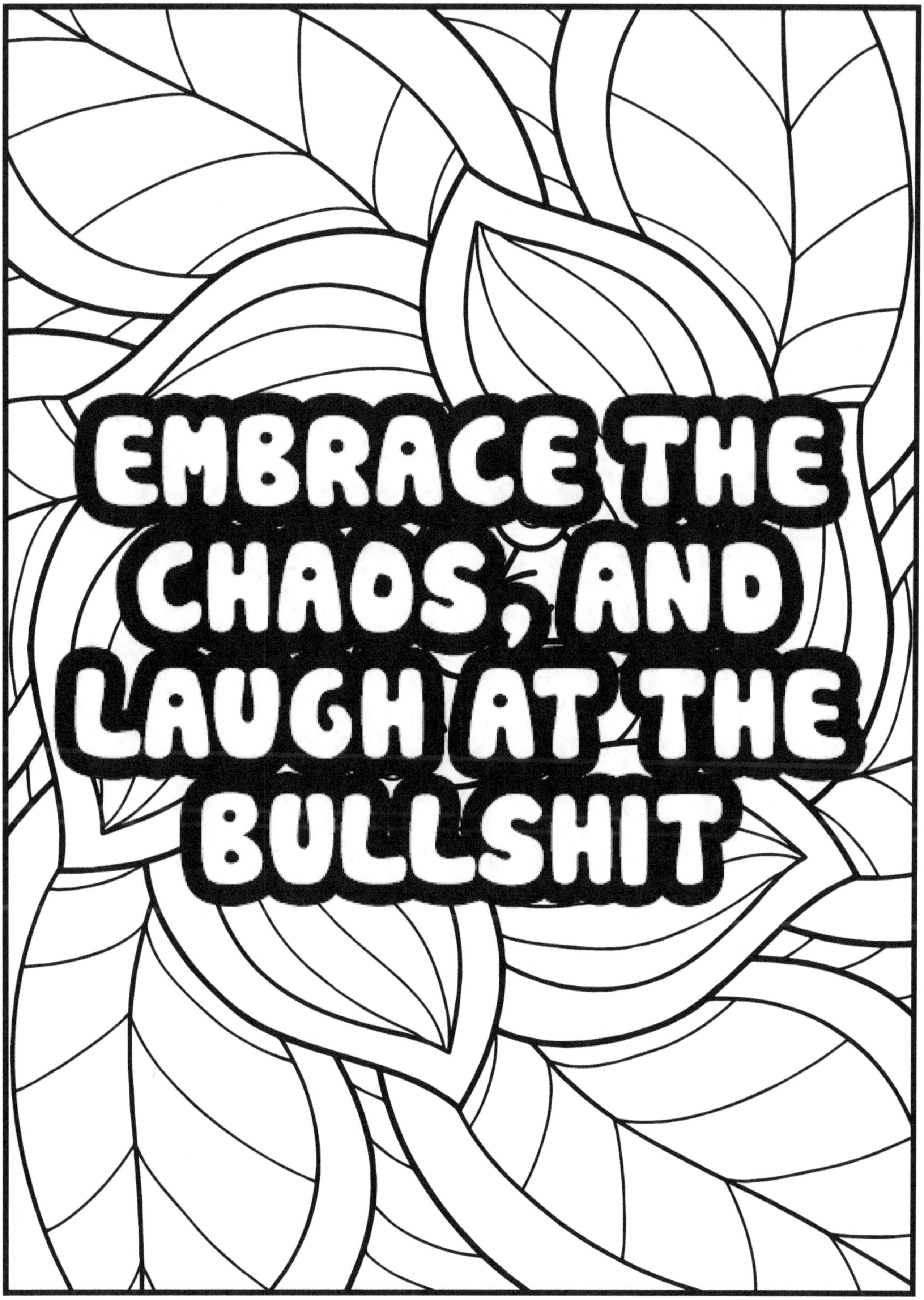
EMBRACE THE
CHAOS, AND
LAUGH AT THE
BULLSHIT

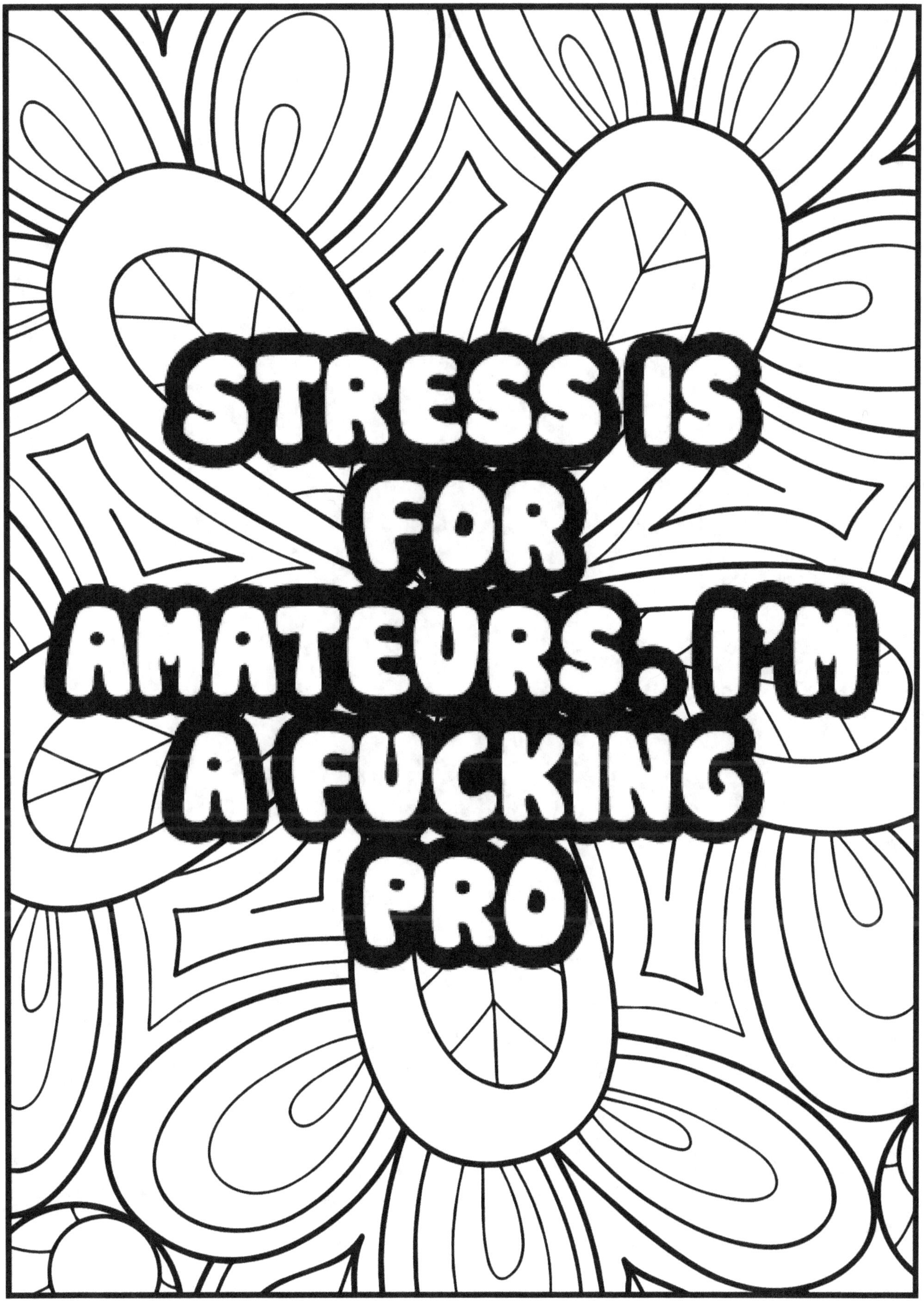
STRESS IS
FOR
AMATEURS. I'M
A FUCKING
PRO

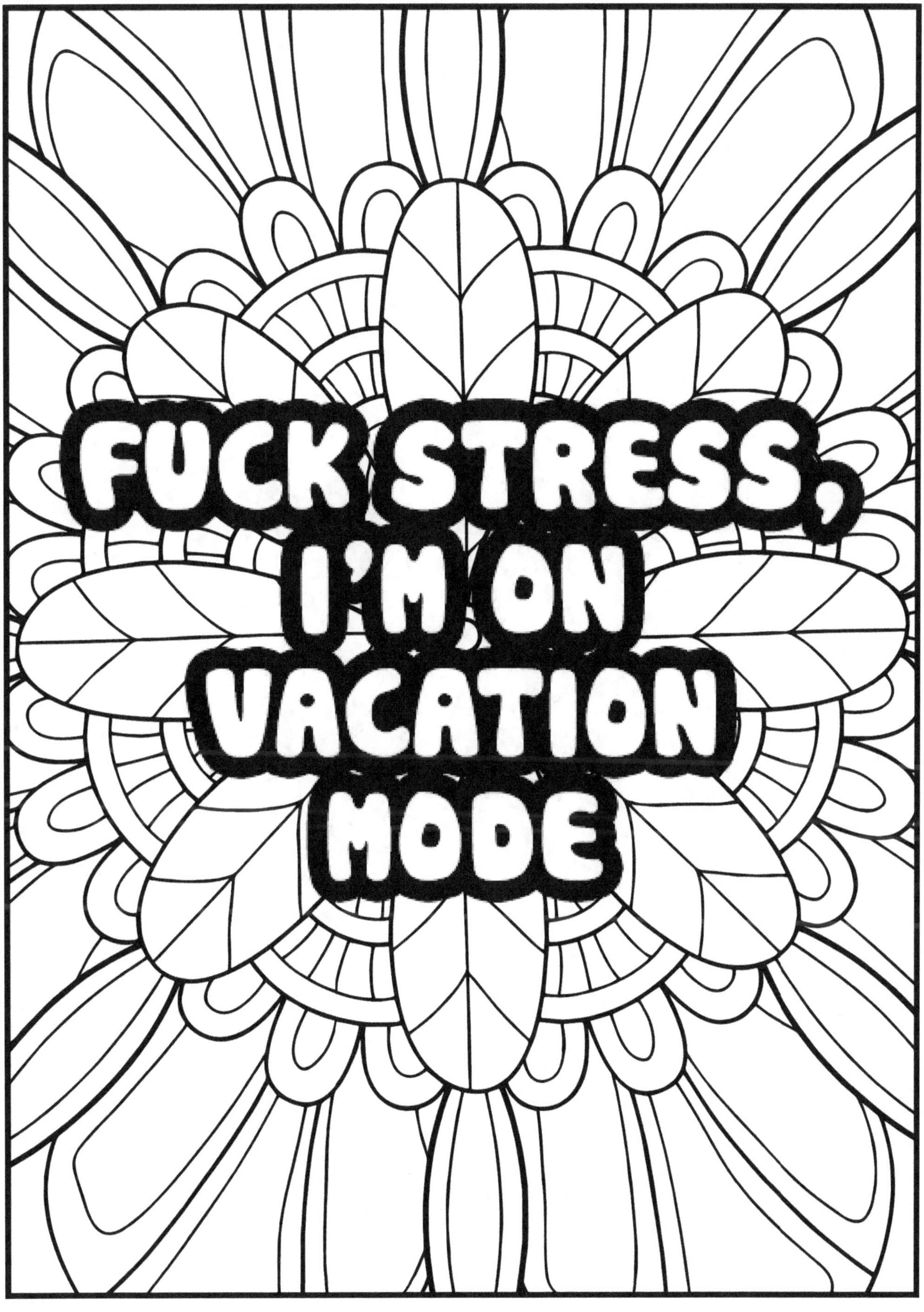
FUCK STRESS,
I'M ON
VACATION
MODE

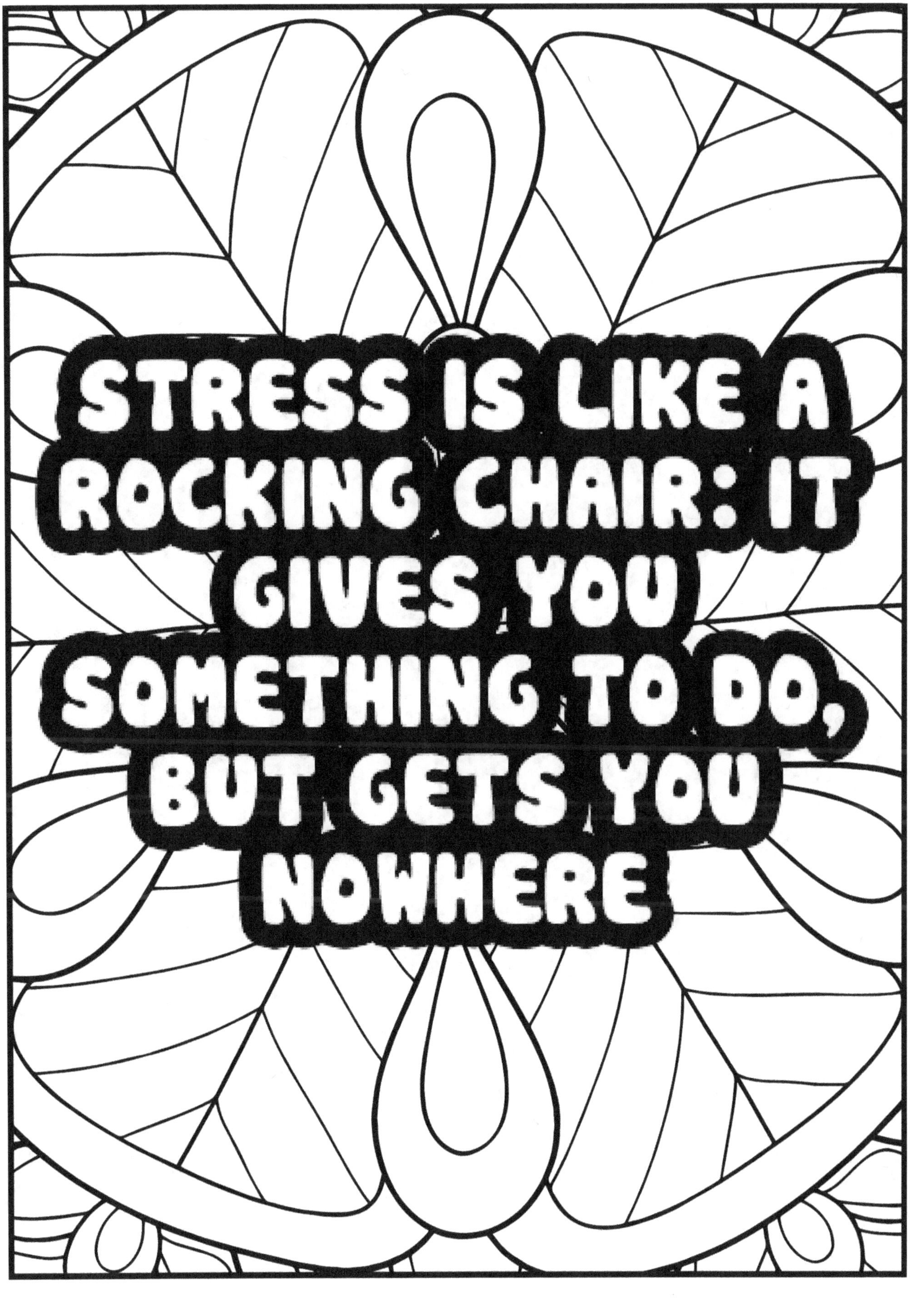
STRESS IS LIKE A ROCKING CHAIR: IT GIVES YOU SOMETHING TO DO, BUT GETS YOU NOWHERE

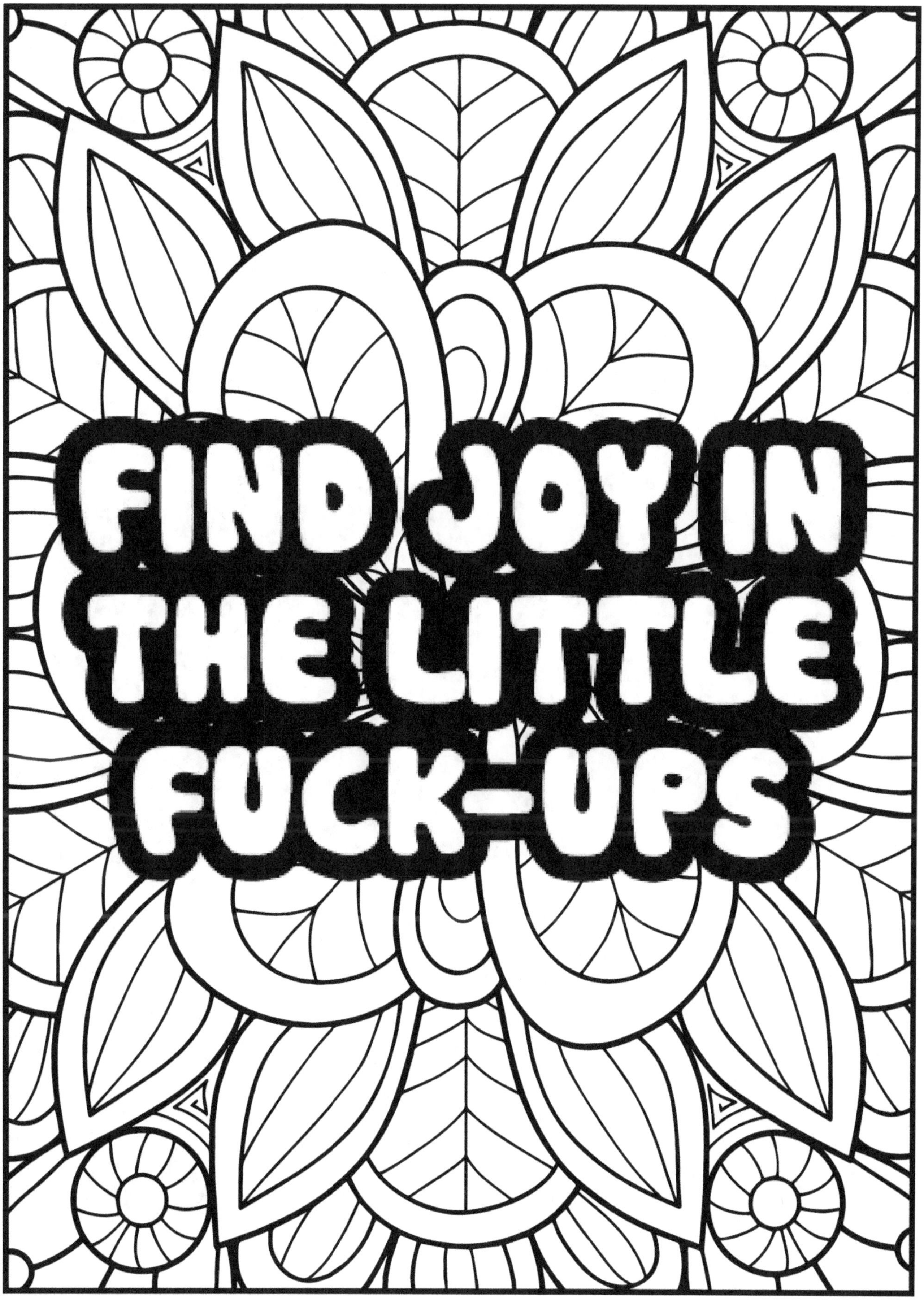
FIND JOY IN
THE LITTLE
FUCK-UPS

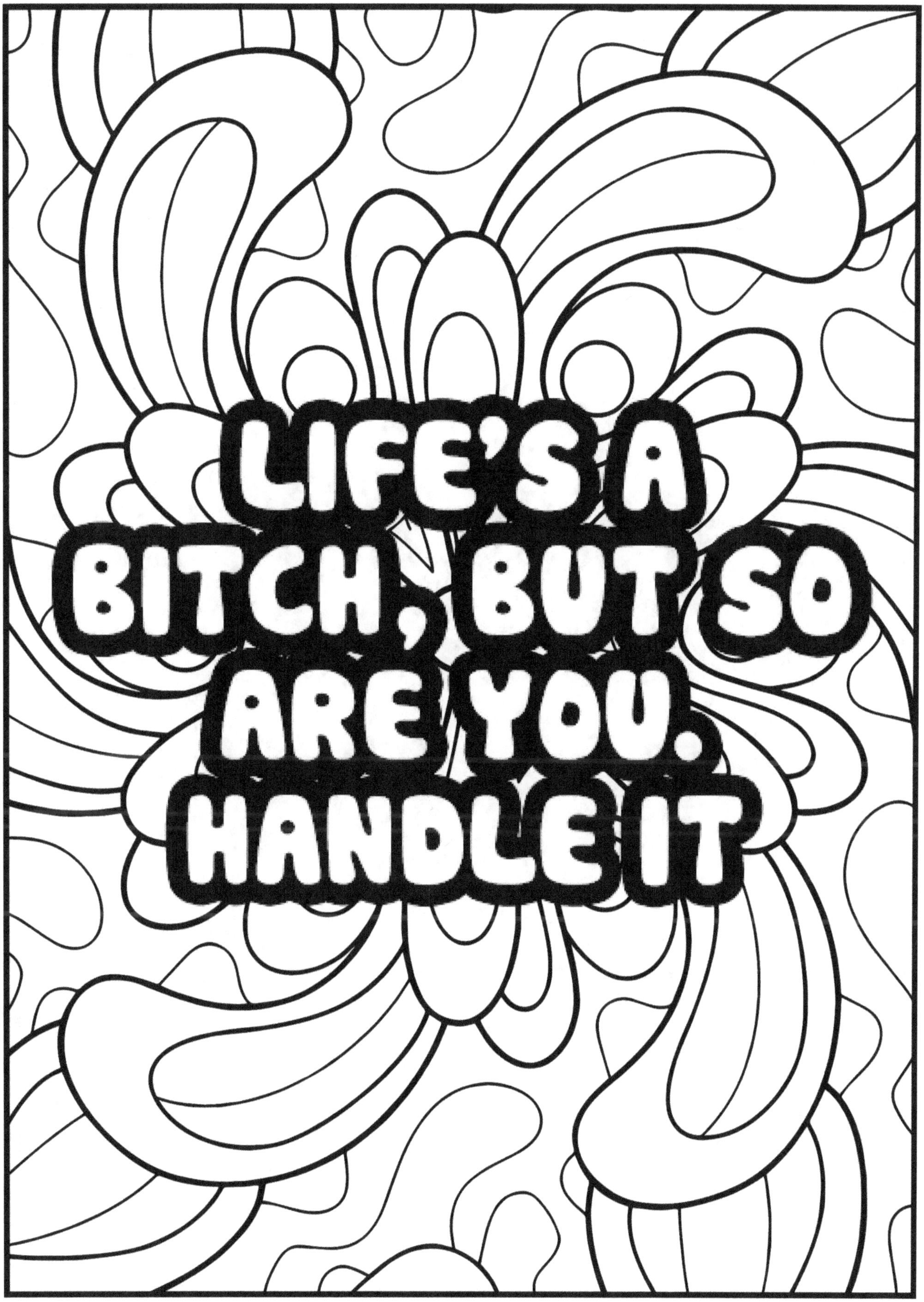
LIFE'S A
BITCH, BUT SO
ARE YOU.
HANDLE IT

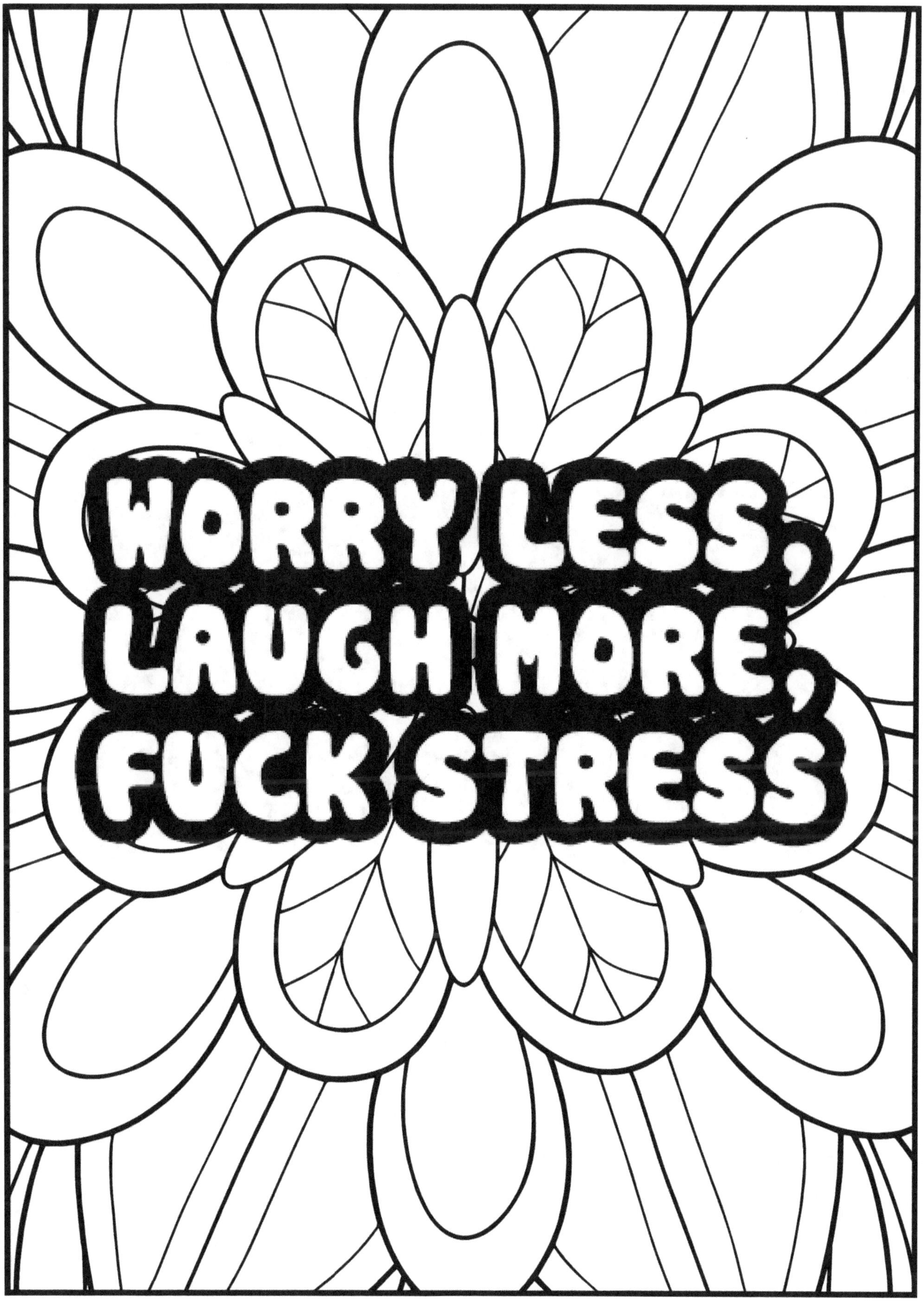
WORRY LESS,
LAUGH MORE,
FUCK STRESS

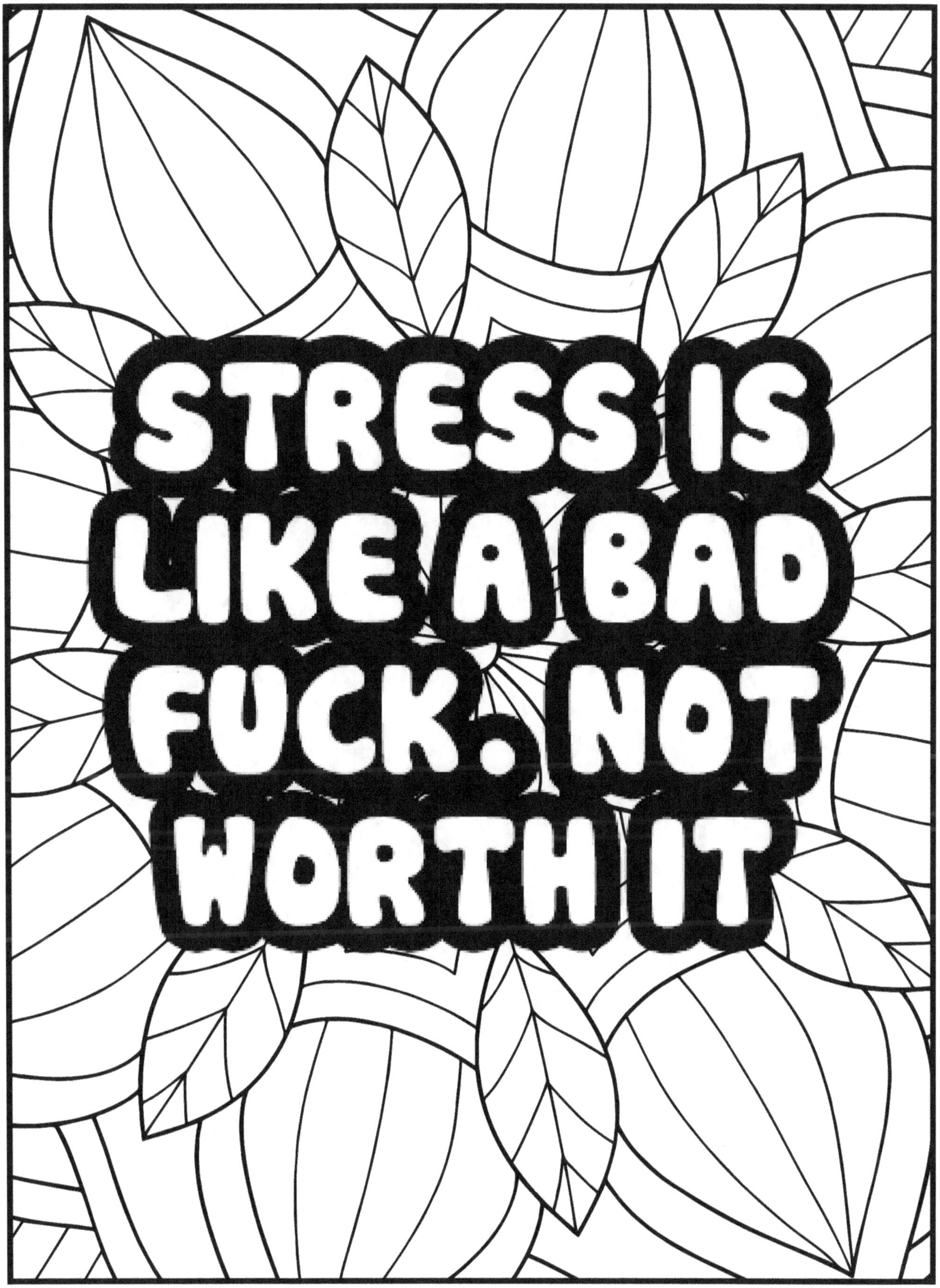
STRESS IS LIKE A BAD FUCK. NOT WORTH IT

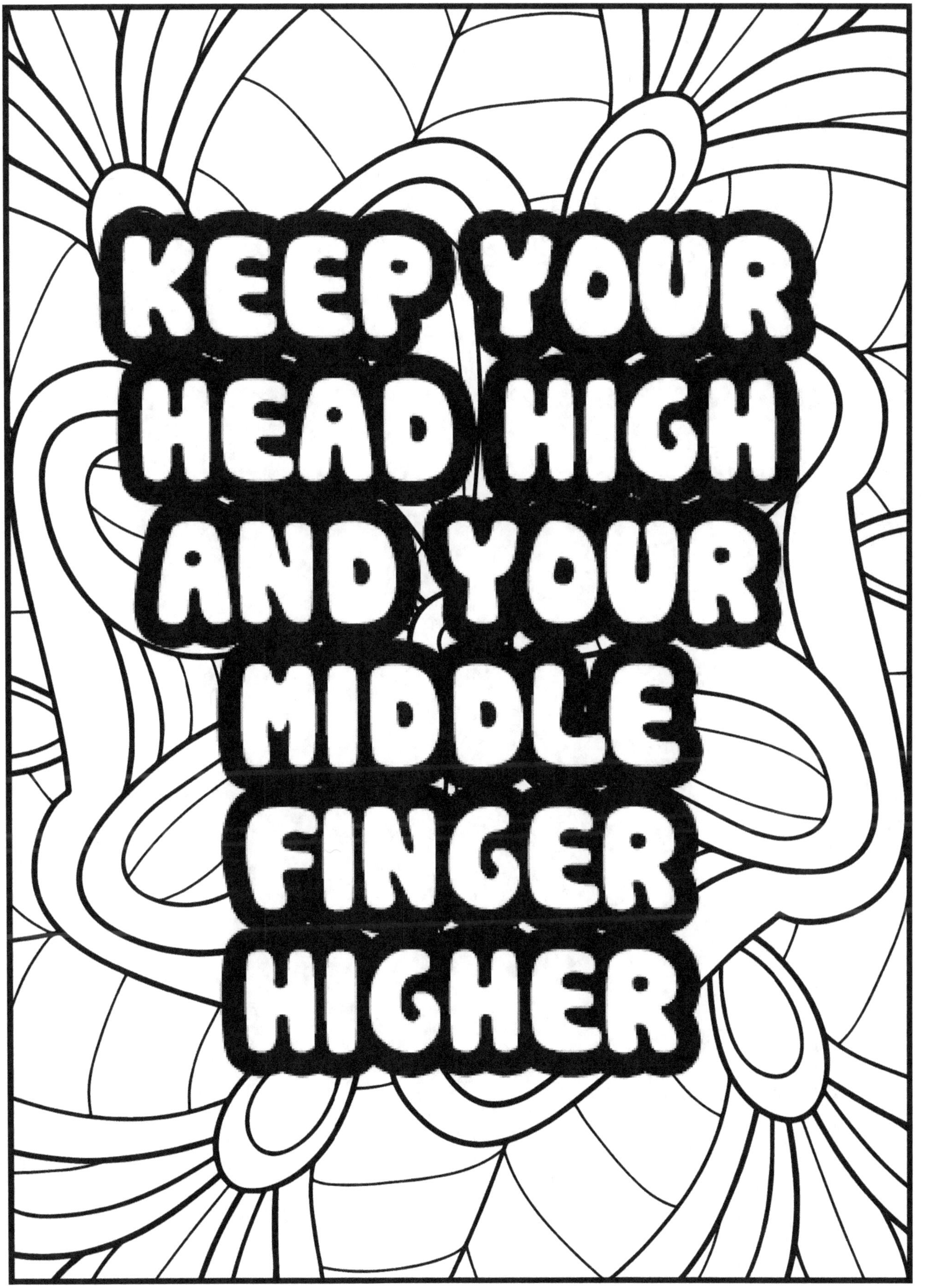
KEEP YOUR
HEAD HIGH
AND YOUR
MIDDLE
FINGER
HIGHER

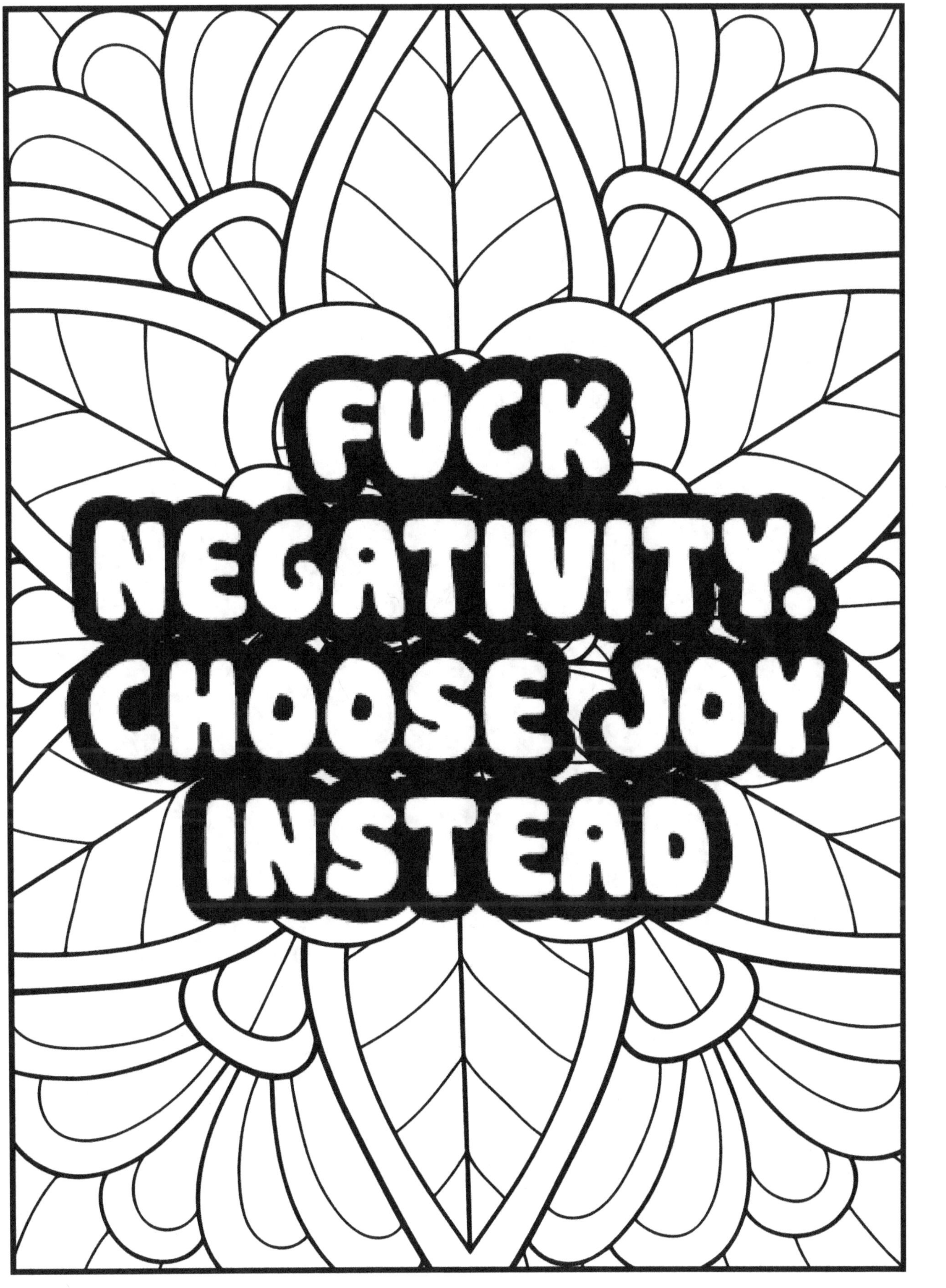
FUCK
NEGATIVITY.
CHOOSE JOY
INSTEAD

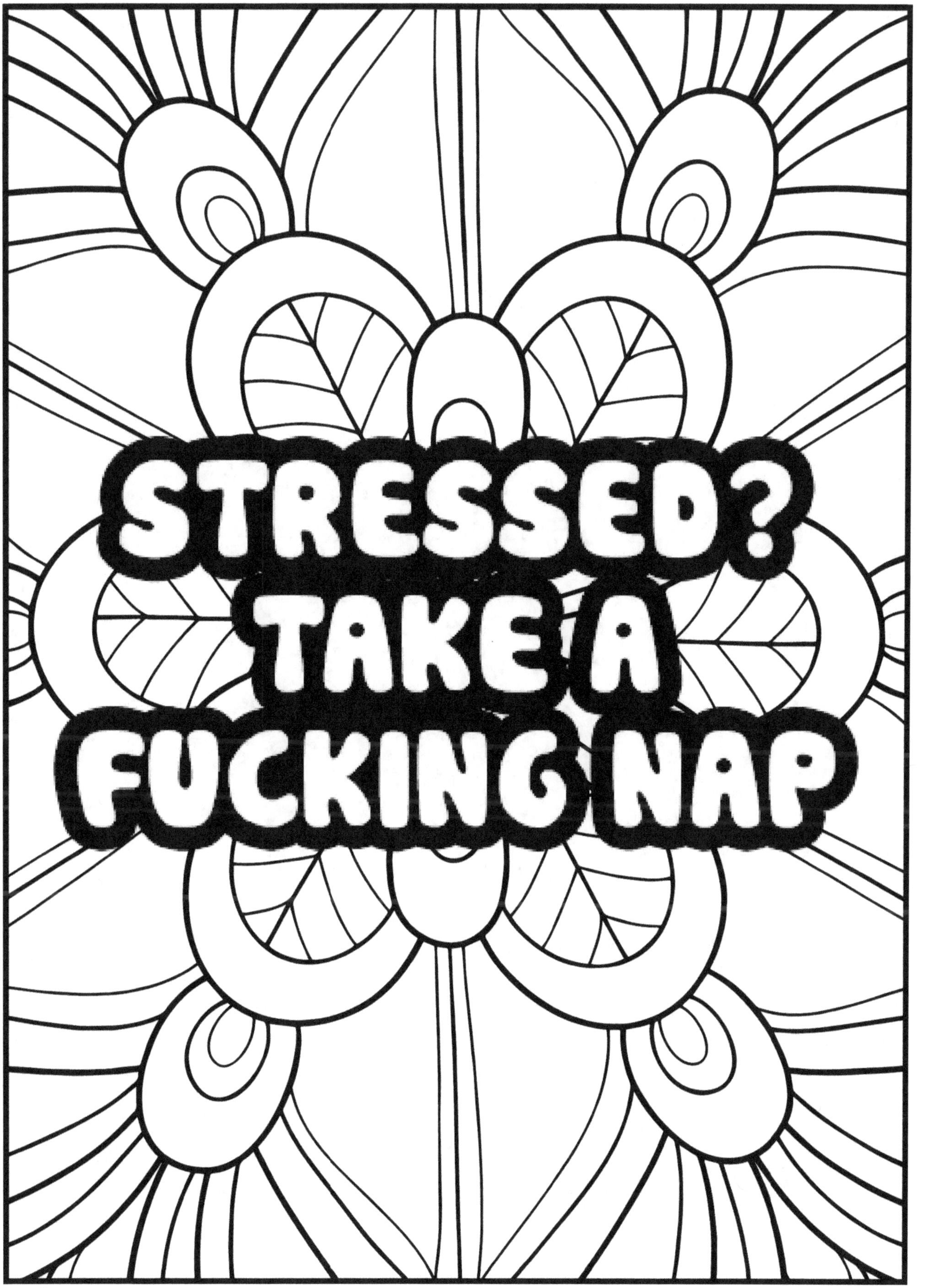
STRESSED?
TAKE A
FUCKING NAP

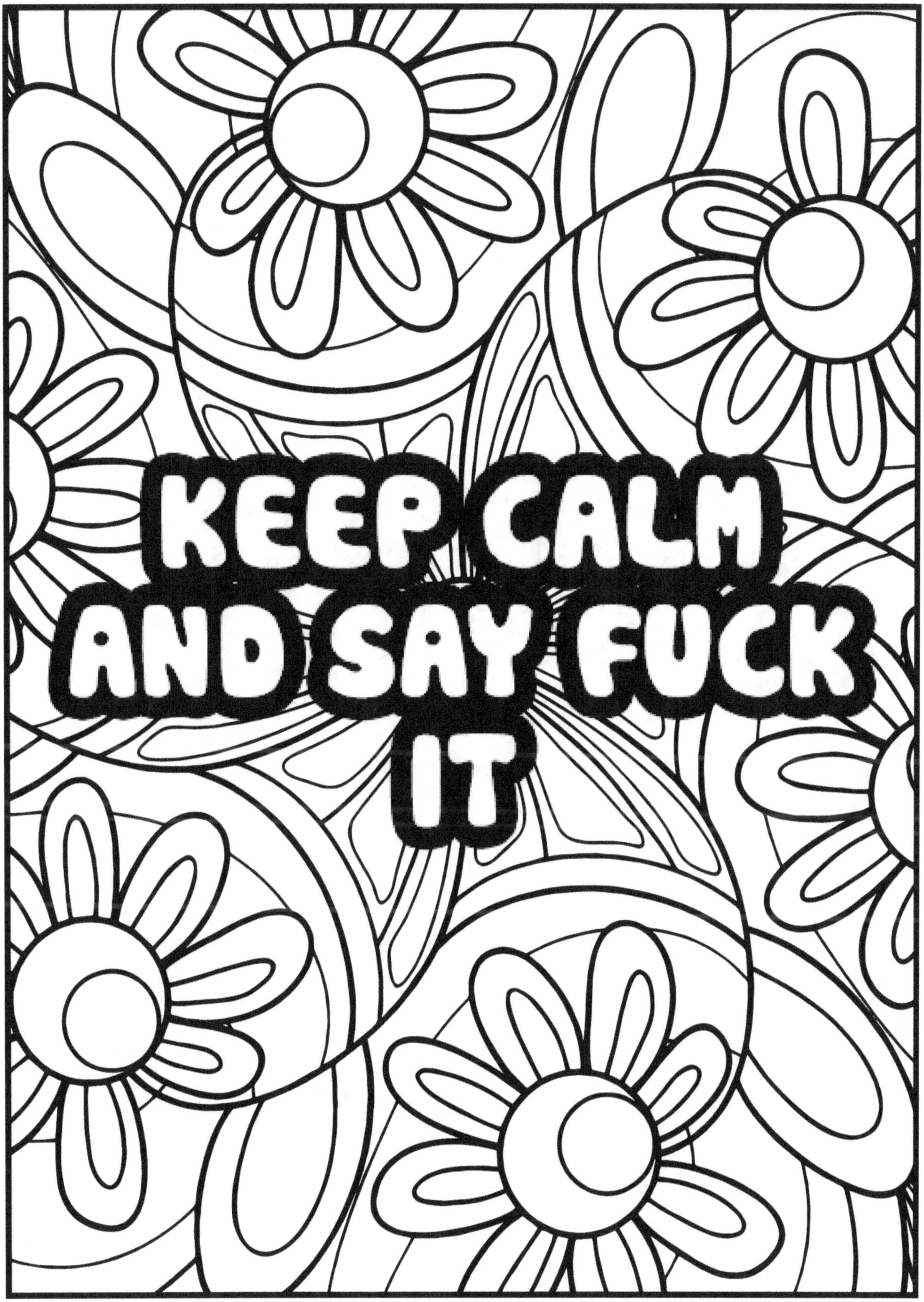
KEEP CALM
AND SAY FUCK
IT

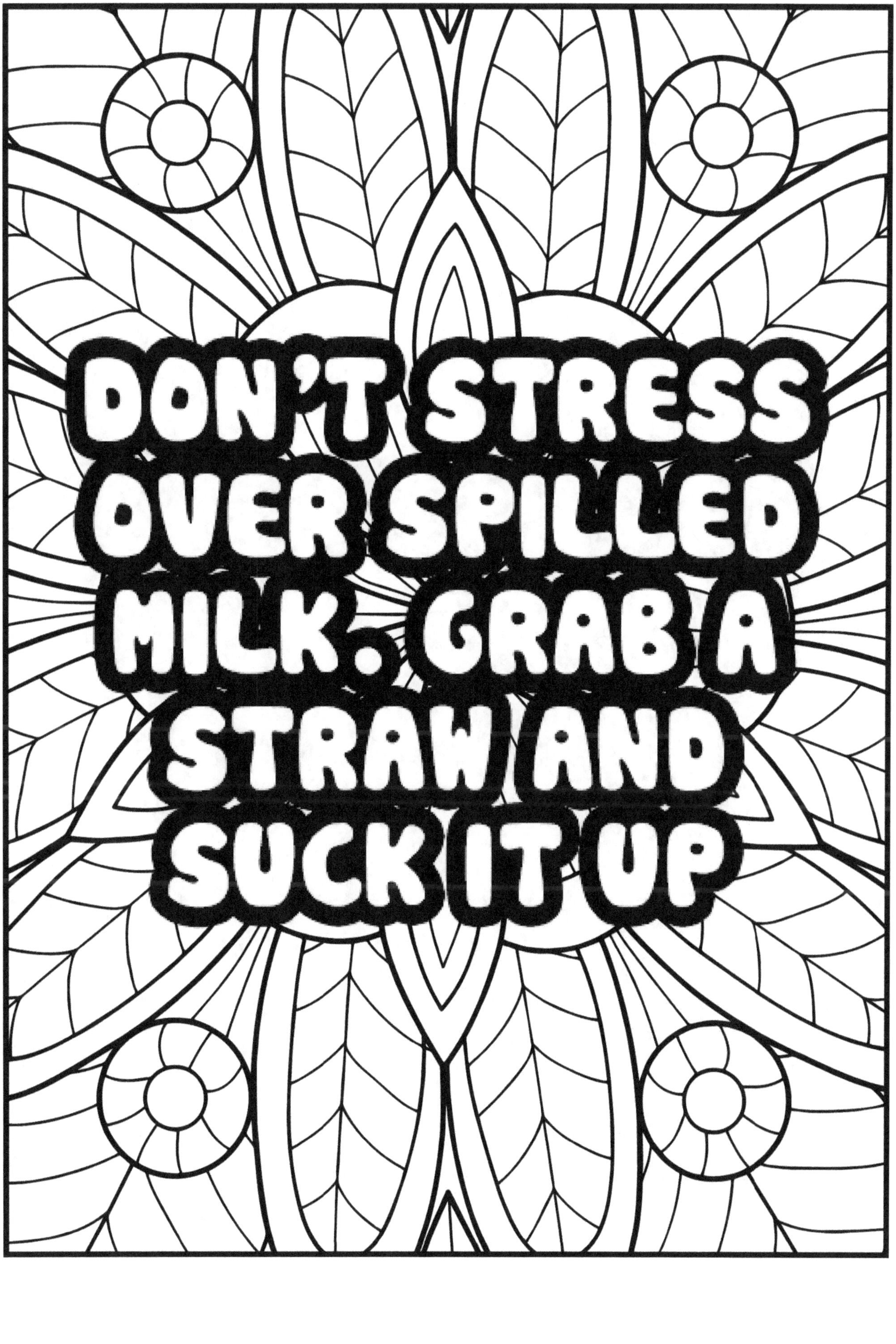
DON'T STRESS
OVER SPILLED
MILK. GRAB A
STRAW AND
SUCK IT UP

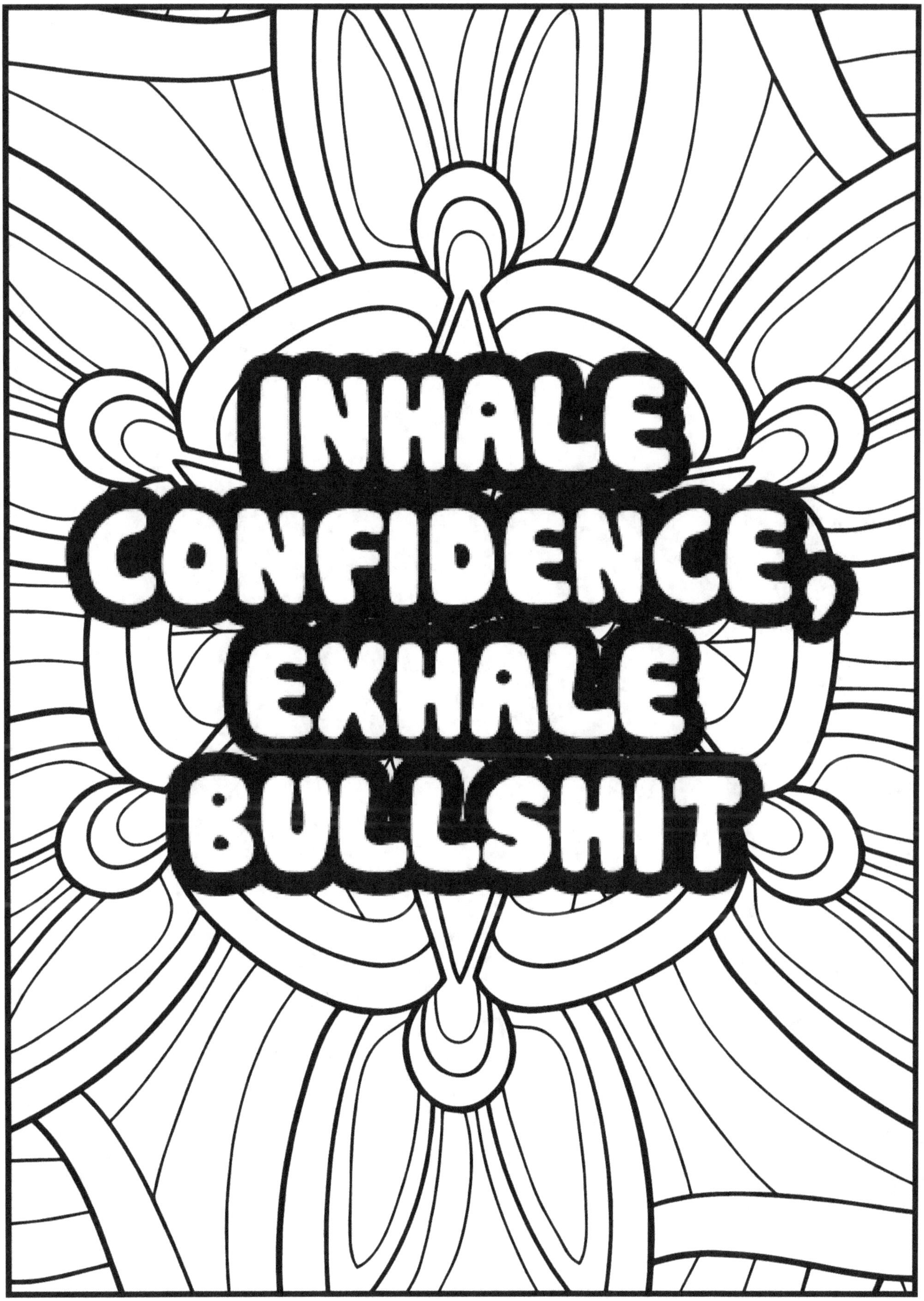
INHALE
CONFIDENCE,
EXHALE
BULLSHIT

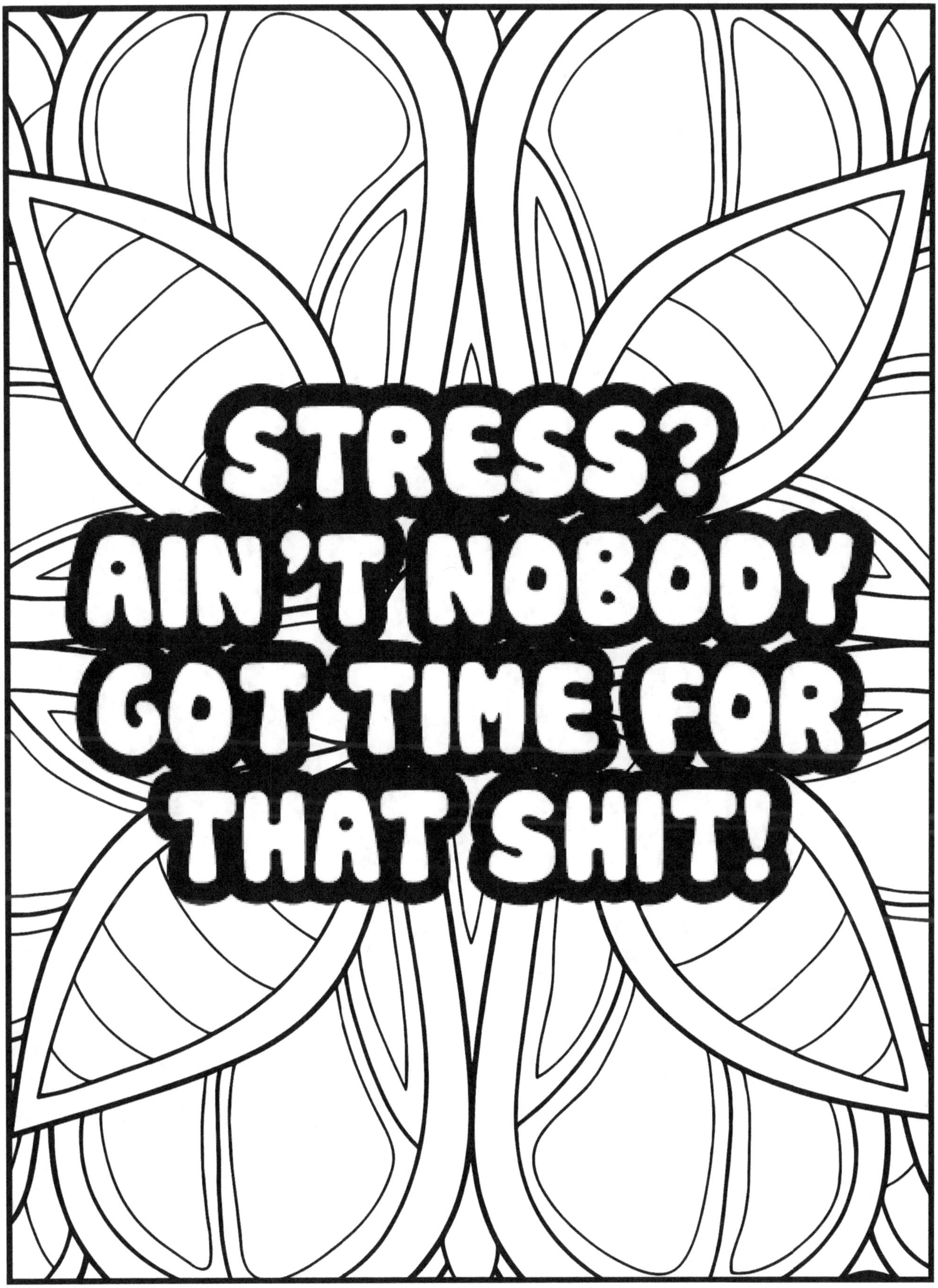
STRESS?
AIN'T NOBODY
GOT TIME FOR
THAT SHIT!

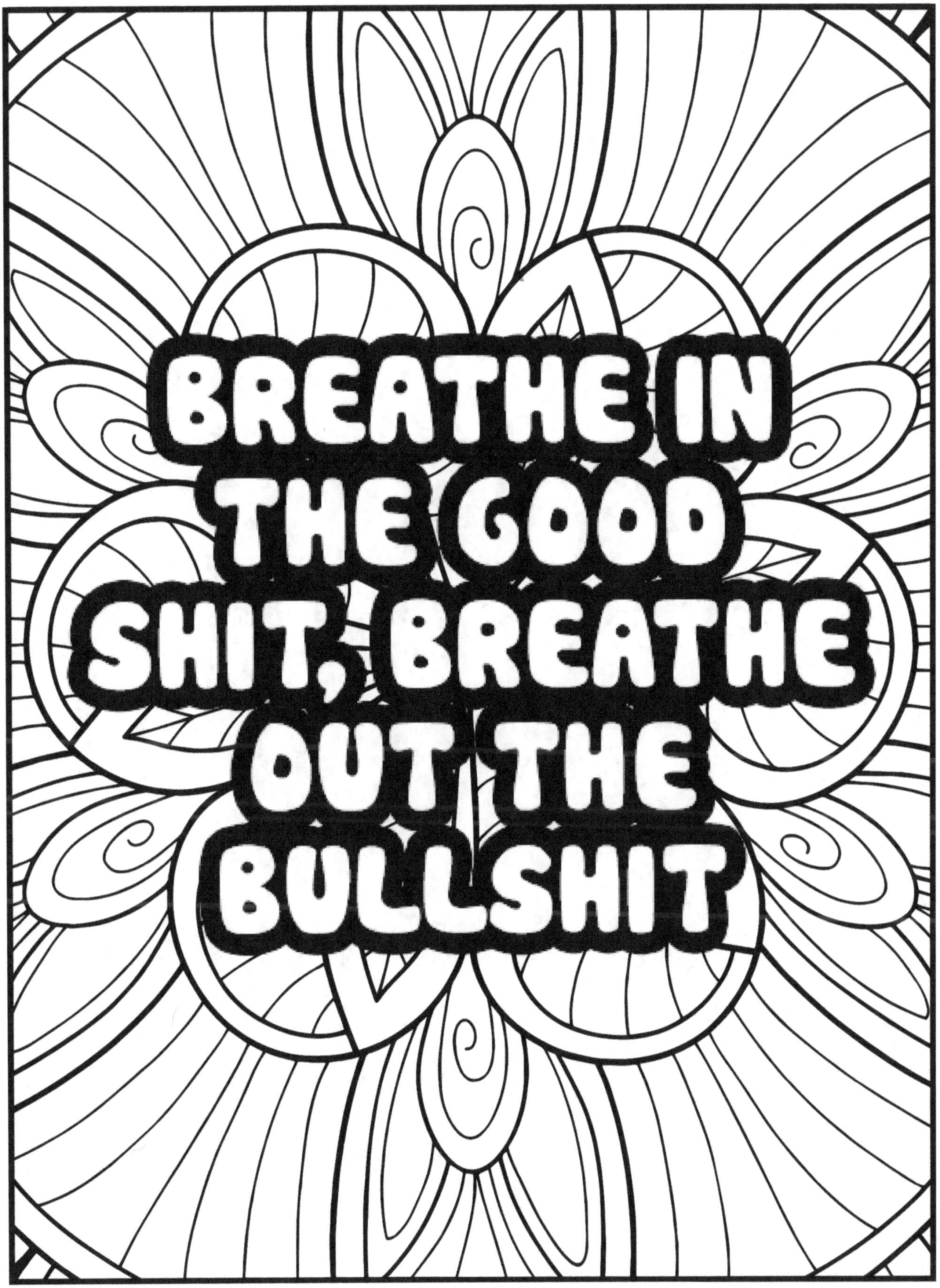
BREATHE IN
THE GOOD
SHIT, BREATHE
OUT THE
BULLSHIT

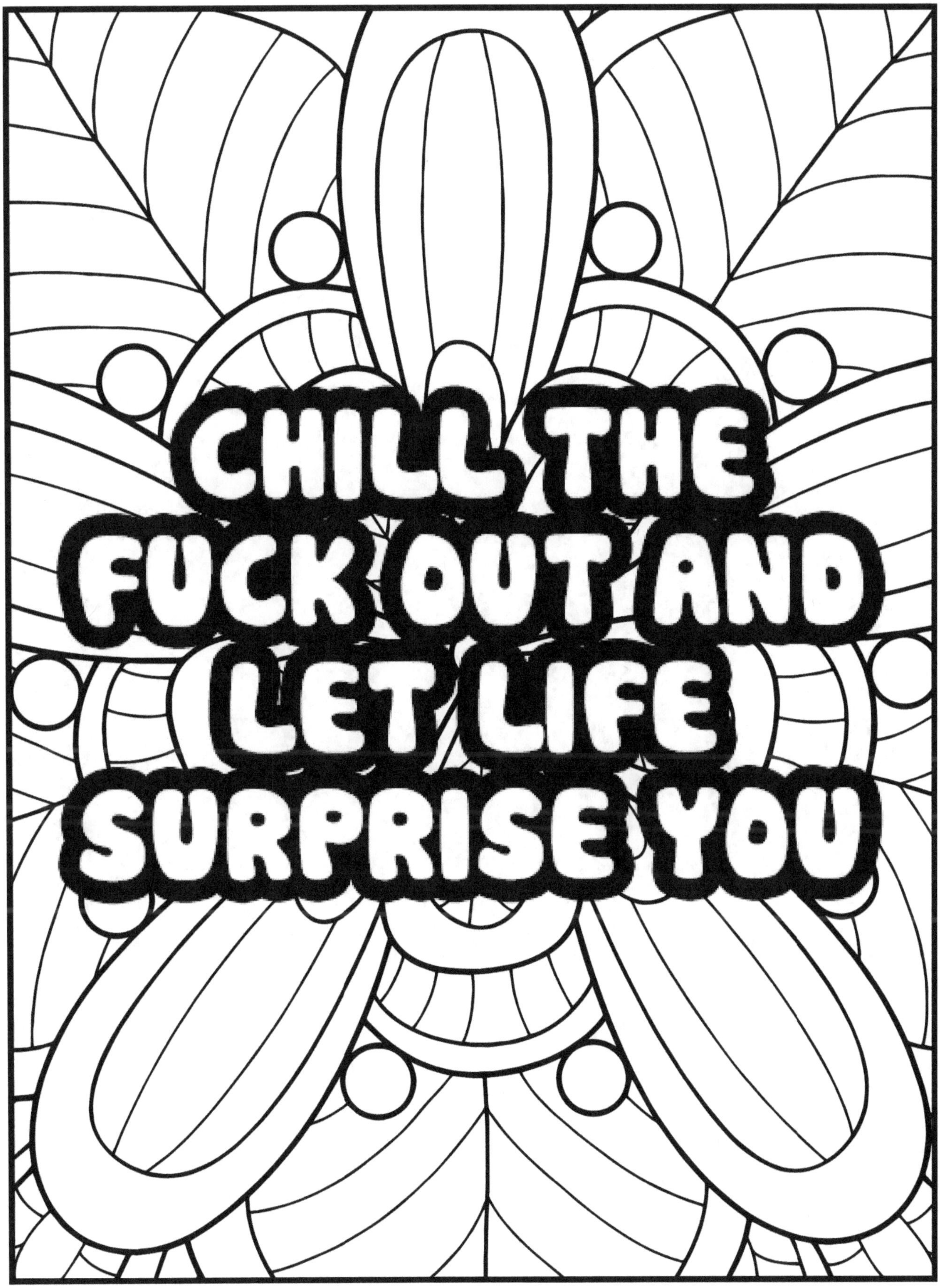
CHILL THE
FUCK OUT AND
LET LIFE
SURPRISE YOU

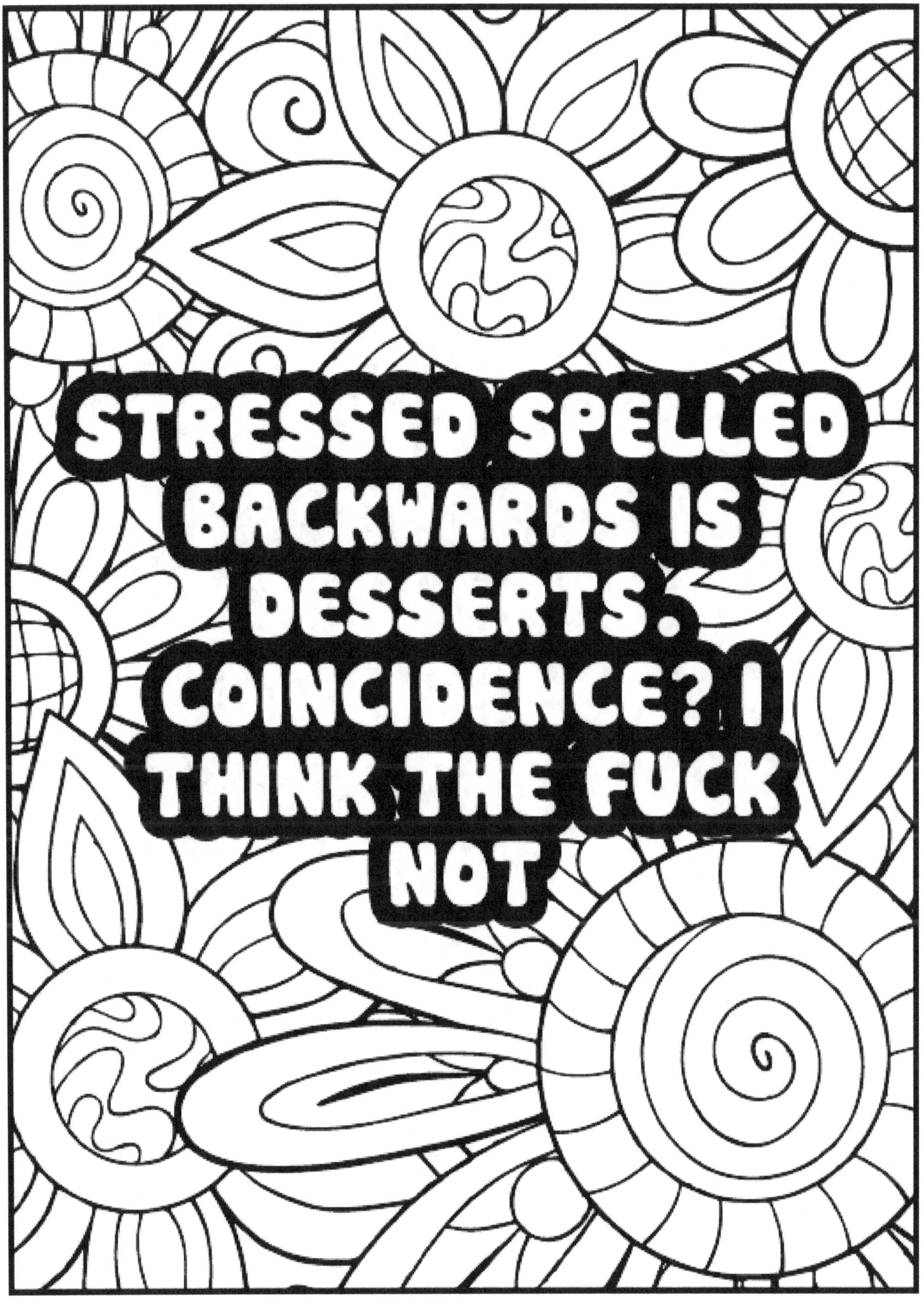
STRESSED SPELLED BACKWARDS IS DESSERTS. COINCIDENCE? I THINK THE FUCK NOT

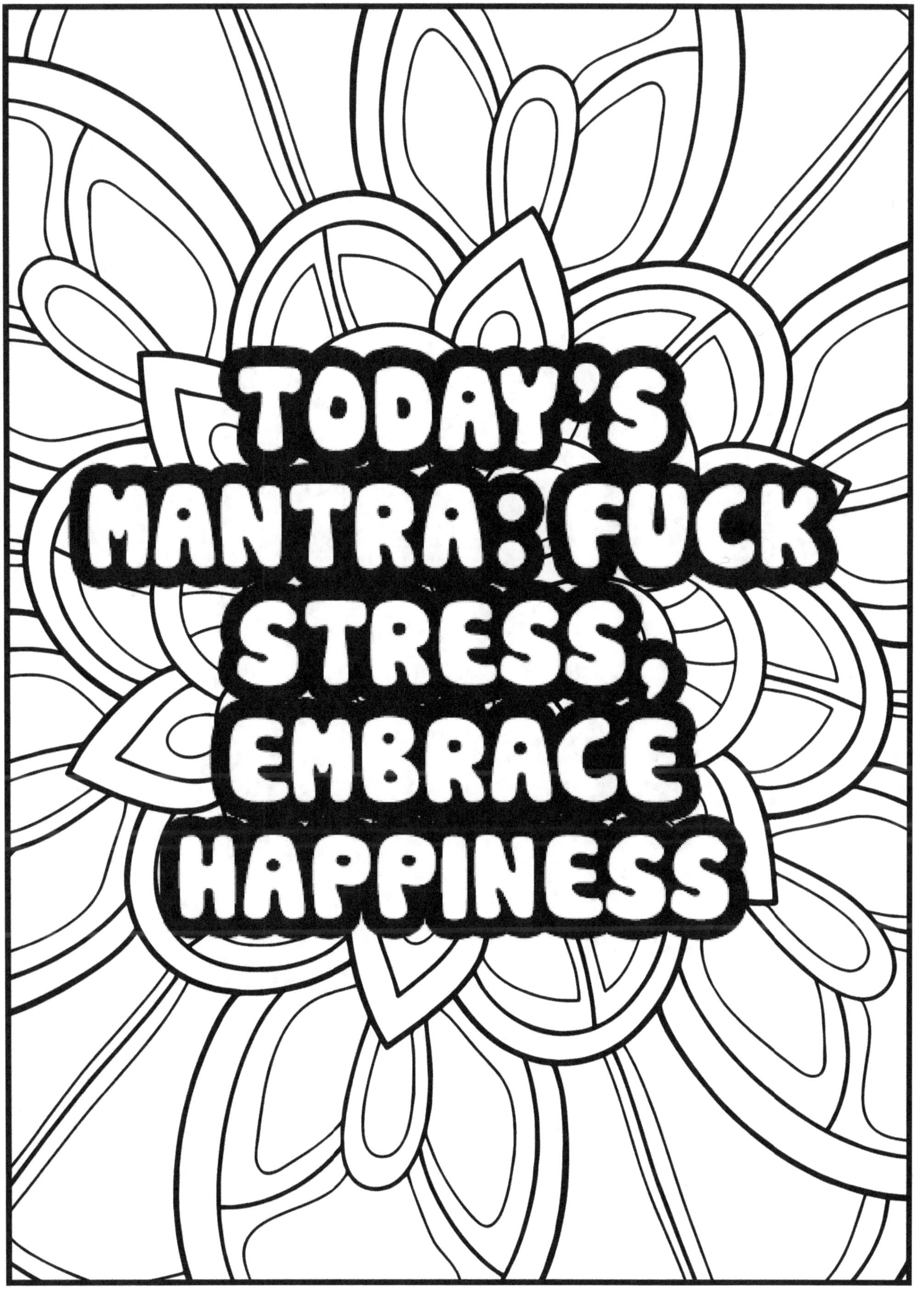
TODAY'S
MANTRA: FUCK
STRESS,
EMBRACE
HAPPINESS

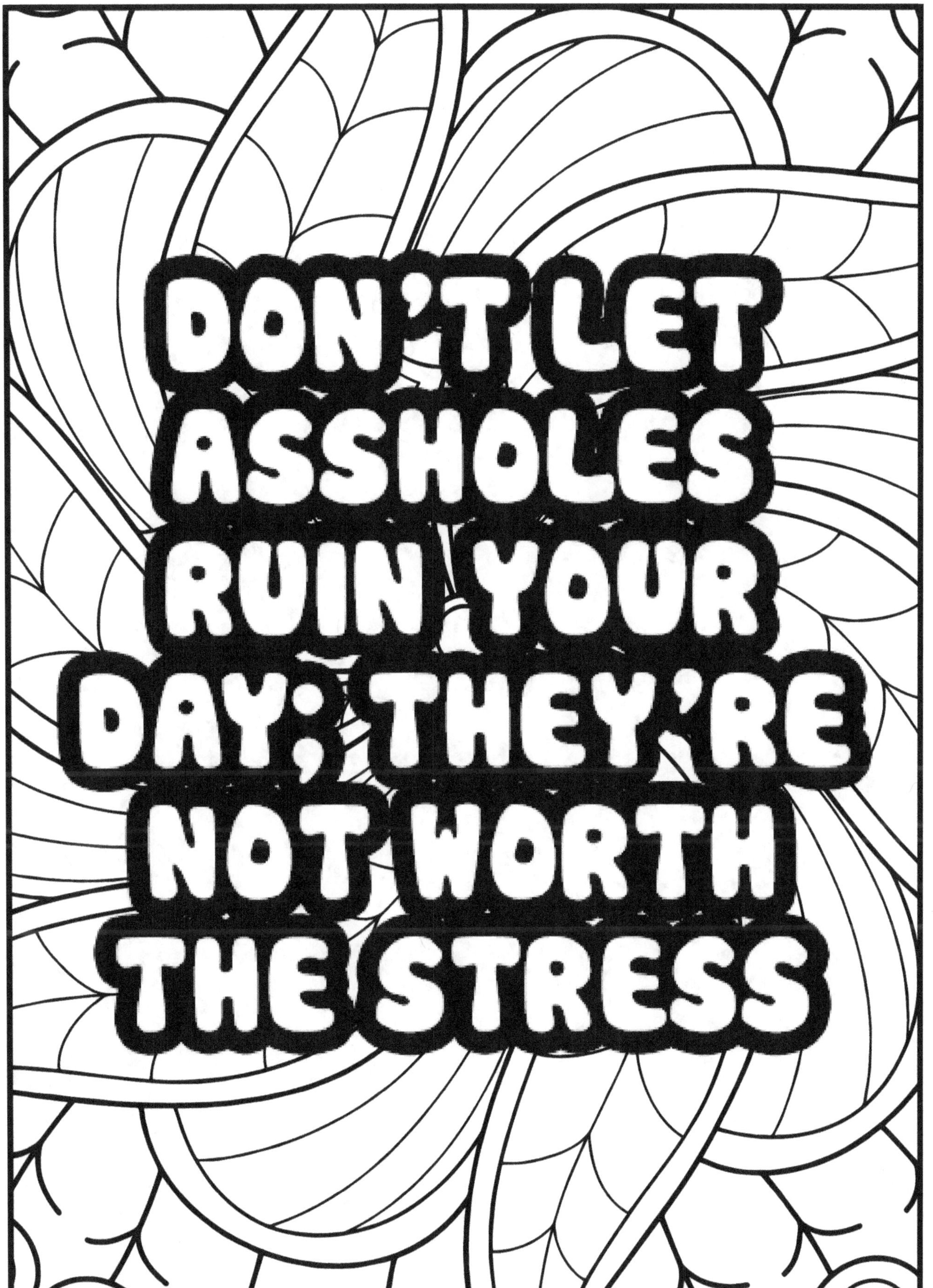
DON'T LET ASSHOLES RUIN YOUR DAY; THEY'RE NOT WORTH THE STRESS

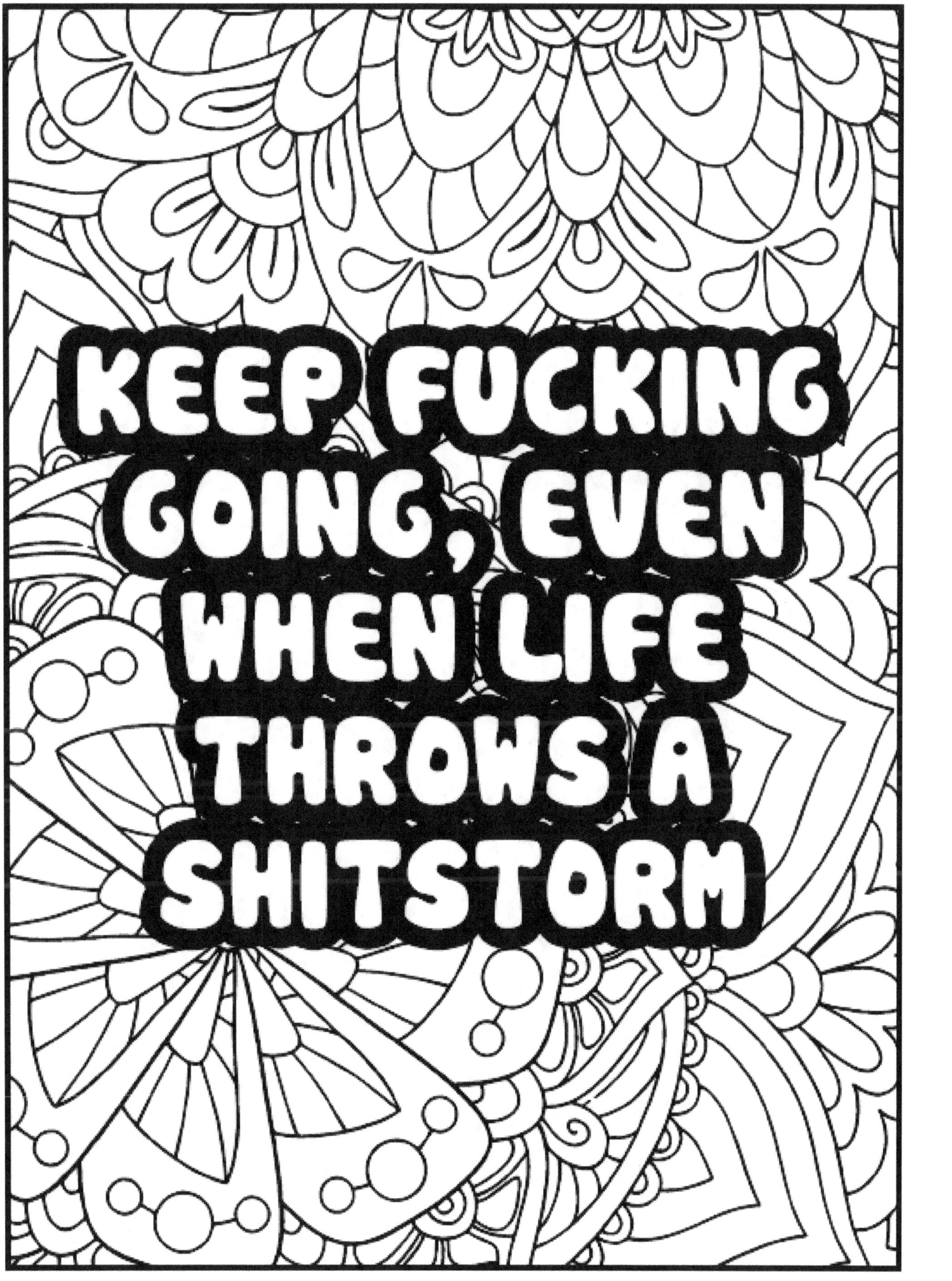
KEEP FUCKING GOING, EVEN WHEN LIFE THROWS A SHITSTORM

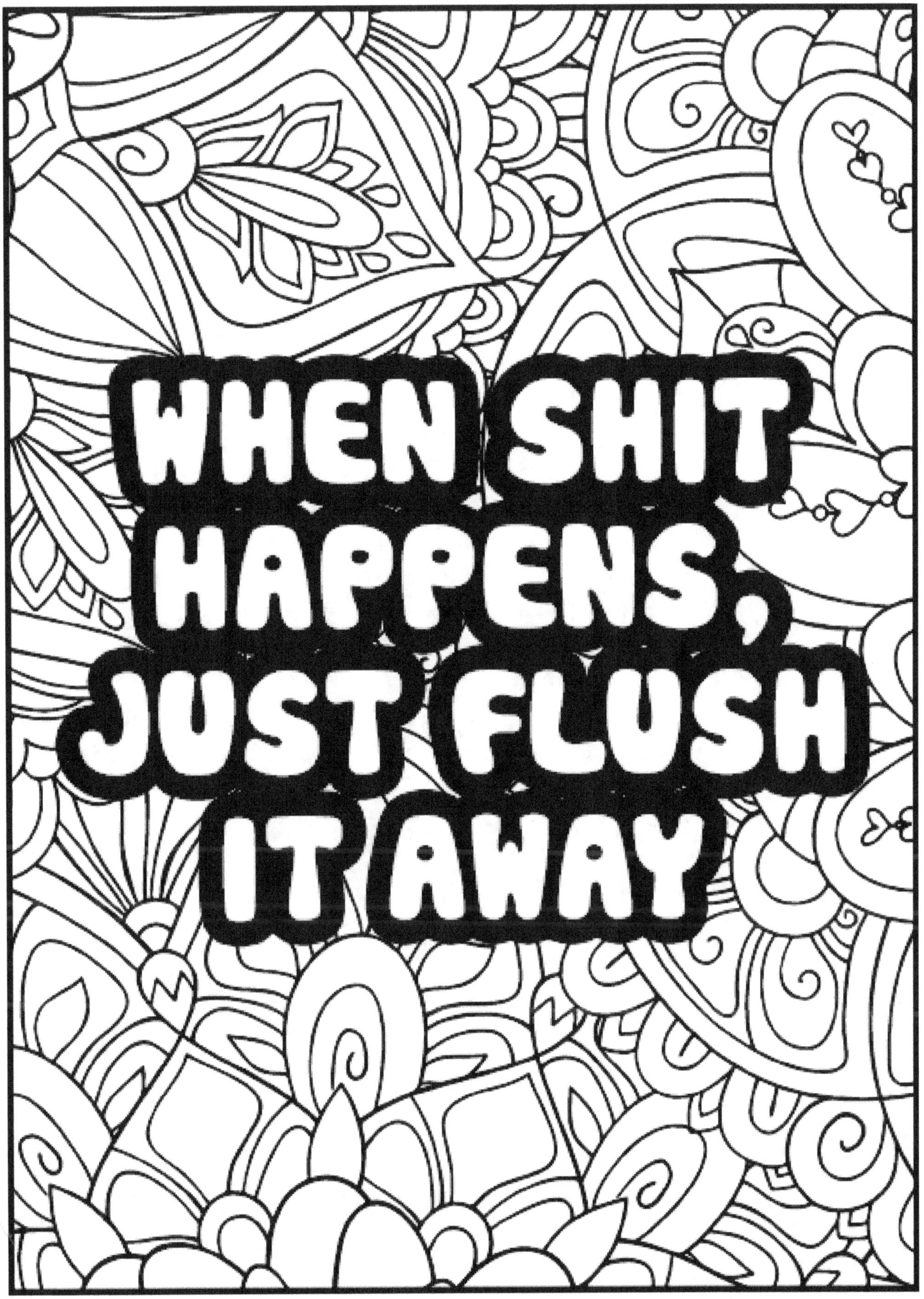
WHEN SHIT
HAPPENS,
JUST FLUSH
IT AWAY

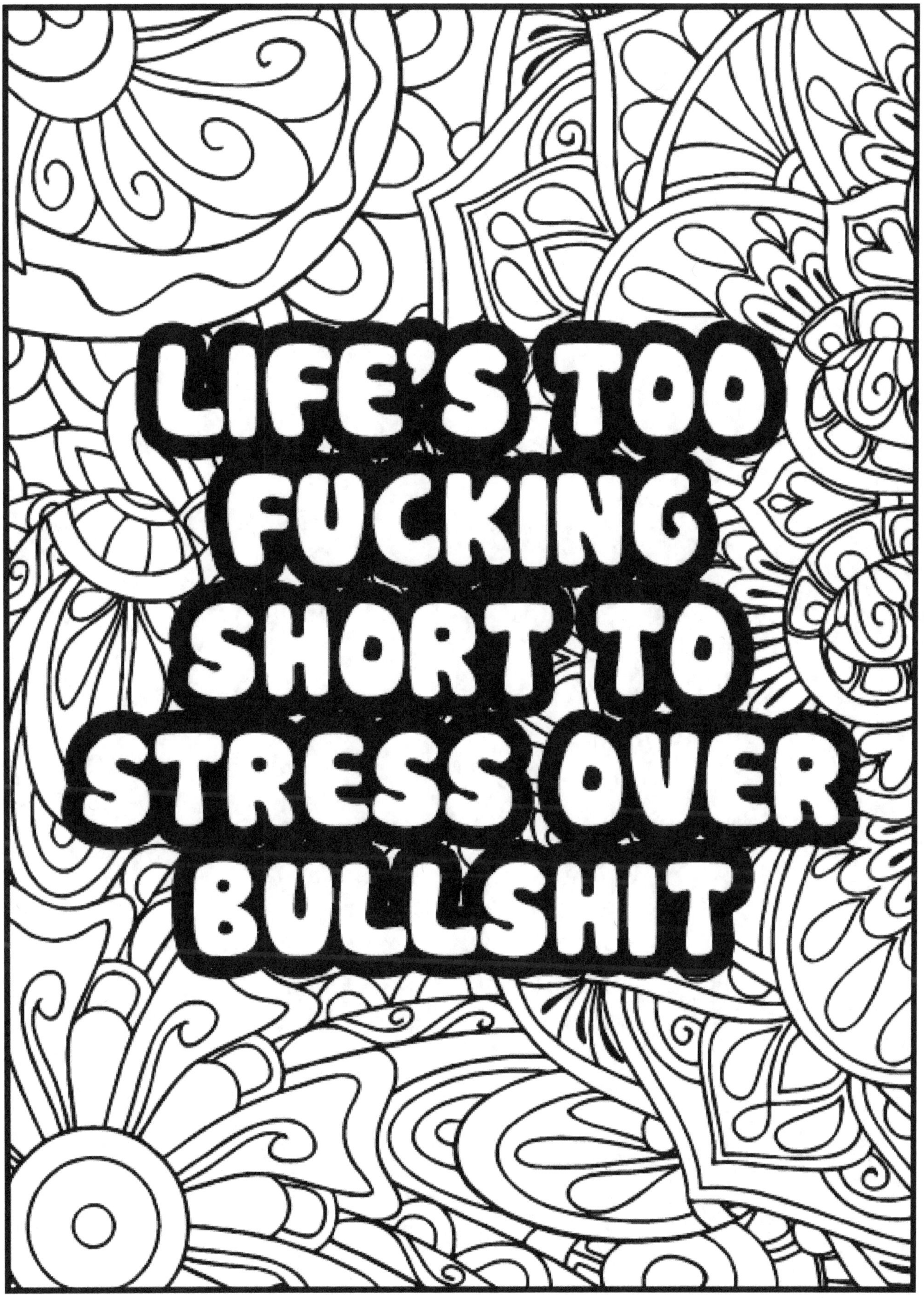
LIFE'S TOO
FUCKING
SHORT TO
STRESS OVER
BULLSHIT

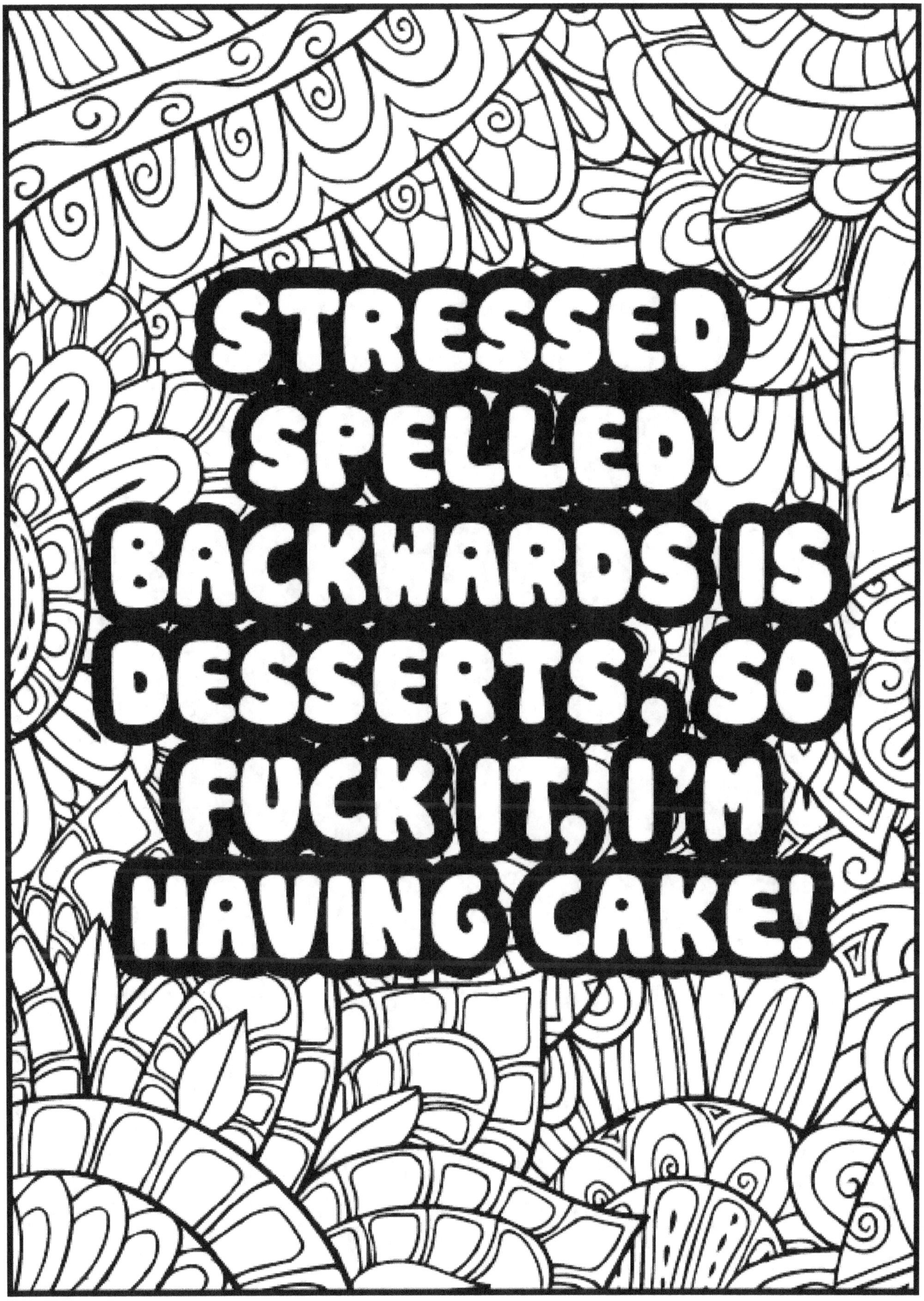
STRESSED SPELLED BACKWARDS IS DESSERTS, SO FUCK IT, I'M HAVING CAKE!

www.ingramcontent.com/pod-product-compliance
Lightning Source LLC
Chambersburg PA
CBHW082212220526
45470CB00010B/3132
* 9 7 9 8 3 2 5 1 9 4 6 9 6 *